To Sue,

END TO END

HOW I CYCLED FROM LAND'S END TO JOHN O' GROATS

With all good wishes,

Christine —

Hope you enjoy the ride!

CHRISTINE GREEN

The right of Christine Green to be identified as the
Author of the Work has been asserted by her in accordance
with the Copyright, Designs and Patents Act 1988.

Editor: Will Rees
Editorial: Shaun Russell

Printed and bound in the UK by
Severn, Bristol Road, Gloucester, GL2 5EU

Published by
Jelly Bean Books
Mackintosh House
136 Newport Road, Cardiff, CF24 1DJ, Wales, UK
www.candyjarbooks.co.uk

ISBN: 978-1-913637-54-5

DEDICATIONS

There are so many people who have, knowingly or not, made the publication of this book possible.

In the world of literature I am very much the "new kid on the block". Well not so much the new kid, but in my 70s I admit to being the older variety. In 2017 I realised an ambition to cycle from Land's End to John o' Groats, totally unsupported, on my electric bike named Piro.

During lockdown I started to write up my diary of my ride. My daughter, Jennifer Scarfe, started to read it, and in her words, "I couldn't put it down, Mum. You must do something about getting it published." She gave me the confidence to think seriously about her suggestion. I then tested out this possibility by asking others to scan over what I had written. I knew that friends Derek Shottin and David Kenny would give a more critical and unsentimental feedback, rather than my daughter piling praise upon her mum! Thanks gentlemen! My brother, Derek Campbell, reported that he had learned a lot more about our family history and Scotland, adding that he found *End to End* an engrossing read. I am indebted to Justine Scouller, of Far Hill Flowers, who phoned me on a Monday morning, full of excitement. "I couldn't do justice to my sentiments by sending you an email. I had to phone to say it was truly inspiring and entertaining, get it published!" Kay Harris and Mary Farmer endorsed all these kind and encouraging words, but how did one get a book published?

Local author Polly Moreland gave me links into the world of publishing but I found all the information on the websites quite daunting. I needed a publisher with whom I could work alongside and with whom I would feel comfortable. Candy Jar Books of Cardiff came up trumps. Their service provided a welcome for new authors, proof reading, editing, including photographs and maps, printing and distribution, everything I wanted and very much needed. Thank you so much, Shaun and Will. I know that without your excellent services I would not be writing this today.

I am indebted to Women V Cancer for granting their permission to use their logo on my book. During my ride I raised over £7000 for this charity and a proportion of sales from this book will be donated to this worthy cause. From when my website opened, there was not a day when a donation was not received. Every donation, no matter how big or small, expressed the same sentiment and support and I am truly grateful, from the humble biscuit being given by a passing school boy, to Green and Co Accountants and Auditors of Cwmbran who sponsored me per mile, not forgetting Michael who helped me out when I had to cope with modern technology.

It felt like Christmas when Cameron McNeish, the renowned Scottish author, broadcaster, mountain walker and authority of outdoor pursuits, agreed to furnish me with a foreword. Thanks a million, Cameron. I was overwhelmed to receive your generous endorsement.

My friend and neighbour, Emily Irwin, was recently diagnosed with breast cancer and could relate to the support which she has benefitted from throughout her contact with one of Women V Cancer charities, "Breast Cancer Now." I truly appreciate your introduction, Emily, especially sharing your personal experience at such a challenging time.

I owe a great deal to the people I became involved with throughout my training: Jennifer Boorer with my pilates, Dawn who monitored me throughout my swimming lessons, Adrian who, after my bike test in the gym told me "you can do it," Phil Chadwick, my neighbour, who has a wealth of cycling experiences and who offered first-hand practical advice. Everyone whom I met en route made my journey memorable and are due recognition, which I hope I have given within these pages.

However, I must mention especially, my daughter Helen Brown, and grandson Thom Brown who were "in on it" from the start. Young Thom accompanied me on many training rides while Helen was my sounding block from when I made my first tentative rumblings about taking on this challenge. She was there for me during my ride, by phone and email, picking me up when the going got tough. As for the most tremendous welcome which she organised at the end of the road...!

En route, my elder daughter, Jennifer, always seemed to send a loving text at the moment I needed it most, not forgetting Amy Scarfe, my granddaughter, for all her witty messages, jokes and emails which I looked forward to every few days.

Most importantly, to my husband Hugh who uttered the words, "I'll take you to the start and collect you at the end and worry about you every day in between." His love, encouragement and belief in me sustained me throughout one thousand miles. He was with me in spirit every pedal of the way. Words are insufficient to say how much this mattered.

Finally, I would like to acknowledge everyone who has bought my book. I really hope that you will enjoy it, and that it may encourage you to realise your dreams. Many things seem impossible, until they are done.

Christine Green, 2021.

FOREWORD

Like me, Christine Green is a born-again cyclist. After a life of climbing hills and mountains I turned to the humble bike to allow me to continue to bikepack instead of backpack, touring long distance routes while still sitting on my backside. And, like Christine, I have become a convert to the e-bike, or pedal-assist bike as I like to refer to it. You still have to work hard, you still have to turn those wheels, but you get a little help in doing so from a tiny electric motor.

What I haven't achieved is a real long-distance tour on my e-bike, but Christine has. You can't get any further in this country of ours than Land's End to John o' Groats, the classic LEJoG, and a wonderful route it is, experiencing all aspects of English and Scottish (and in my case a wee bit of Wales too) landscapes and the sheer diversity of people and places we have in both nations.

Christine has documented both those aspects of our land in her book and in doing so has helped raise the profile of Women V Cancer. More so, she has proved that with determination, hope and vision, reaching the proverbial three score years and ten needn't signal the end of an active life.

Cameron McNeish, 2021.
Mountaineer, cyclist and author.

INTRODUCTION

Christine's LEJoG journey at seventy is a brilliant reminder to us that, whatever age and commitments back home, you can always drop it all and take up a challenge you have plotted many times in your head. She shows us that pushing the boundaries often makes us feel most alive and connected to the people around us. Christine's cycle ride of over one thousand miles taking in the heart of urban Manchester as well as the peaks of the Slaidburn stage, is one of inspirational endurance and camaraderie that made her feel: "full of health, energy and hopes for the future". When, during the peak of Covid-19 I was diagnosed with breast cancer, it was words such as Christine's that spurred me on.

Christine raised a staggering amount for Women V Cancer, not only from friends and family back home, but from passers-by along LEJoG who were also inspired by her tenacity and enthusiasm. One of Women V Cancer's few selected charities, Breast Cancer Now, has really helped me decode the complicated terms and treatments for breast cancer. At medical appointments I felt informed to ask the right questions for my particular case, due to Breast Care Now's clear and well explained information. Their Breast Care nurses are also at the end of a line to answer the most challenging of questions. A percentage of the profits from the sale of the book will be given to Women V Cancer who do an invaluable job of supporting women like me.

Having descended the peak of cancer treatment, I'm inspired by Christine to cycle LEJoG route (with a small electric motor of course), and I'll be armed with her book that is at once a practical guide, a history, a personal journey and above all an engaging and motivating read.

Where will she go next?

Emily Irwin, 2021.

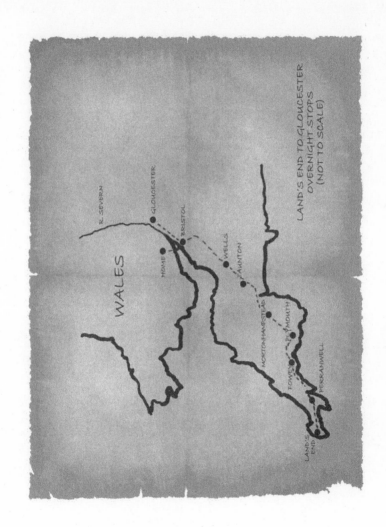

LAND'S END TO GLOUCESTER
OVERNIGHT STOPS
(NOT TO SCALE)

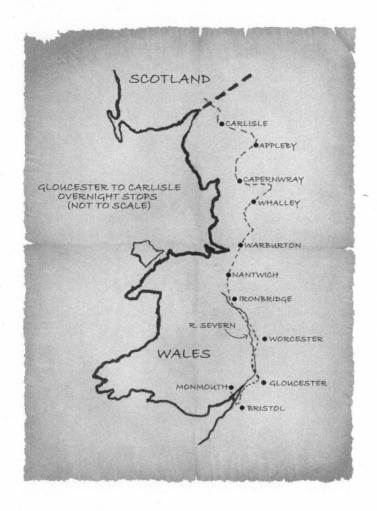

SCOTLAND

●CARLISLE

●APPLEBY

●CAPERNWRAY

GLOUCESTER TO CARLISLE
OVERNIGHT STOPS
(NOT TO SCALE)

●WHALLEY

●WARBURTON

●NANTWICH

●IRONBRIDGE

R. SEVERN

WALES

●WORCESTER

MONMOUTH● ●GLOUCESTER

●BRISTOL

4

JOHN O'GROATS
MELVICH
ALTNAHARA
INVERAN
INVERNESS (MAIN TOWN ONLY)
GREAT GLEN
CARRBRIDGE
NEWTONMORE
PITLOHRY
KILLIN
BALLOCH
R.CLYDE
HAMILTON
ABINGDON
LOCKERBIE
CARLISLE

OVERNIGHT STOPS
IN SCOTLAND
(NOT TO SCALE)

PROLOGUE

It would take me another sixty years before I realised the meaning of this word 'adventure'. Were my ten-or-eleven-year-old dreams just a preparation for true adventures in years to come? At this age I could hardly imagine my life in a year's time, let alone sixty!

Some believe that their zodiac sign reflects their personality. I think that there is some truth in this. I am a Scorpio, with *nothing* of adventure featuring in my personality. However, a Scorpio's most well known characteristics are, apparently, determination and passion, along with being brave, loyal and ambitious. If my personality, as interpreted by my star sign, is to be believed then 'I know what I want, I am not afraid to work hard and play hard to get it' – besides which I am credited with being 'seductive and beguiling'! Well, this is what my star sign decrees!

My attributes would, sixty years hence, all play a part in my great adventure. When I went to Mallorca to concentrate on serious training, did I ever imagine that I would overcome one day's obstacles by illicitly joining in the peloton of four thousand cyclists... yes, really! Into the peloton I slipped, unnoticed, to single-mindedly achieve my goal.

Throughout my one thousand miles, I drew upon all the positive and negative attributes of my sign, needing every ounce of stubbornness and determination as I battled into relentless icy rain and supernatural wind, which left me sapped of all energy and in tears. As I pedaled over Dartmoor on my heavy bike, my electric motor started to fail me, and my legs turned to jelly as I endeavoured to conquer the hills without battery assistance.

The loyal, softer side of my sign was evidenced when the gods looked down favourably upon me and decreed that, although I had broken down, I was on the doorstep of the best bike repair shop I could have wished for; I have supported this business ever since, although it is miles away from my home. Then there was the time I gatecrashed a funeral wake and ended up comforting one of the mourners.

On hot days, when melting tar clung to my shoes and climbs left me gasping for breath, I questioned my sanity for having undertaken such a mad adventure – what sometimes felt like a suicide mission. But surely only a scorpion, known for bravery and confronting danger, could face down two masked men carrying guns in a remote part of the Scottish Highlands. My 'controlling' element, meanwhile, came in handy when standing up to rude guest house owners.

But what about the seductive and beguiling bit?

When my bike broke down and a gentleman stopped his car, asking if I would like to spent the night with him, was he drawn to my state of distress or a twinkle in my eye? Come off it, I was a seventy-year-old gran, who was going to have designs on me? Not to mention he assured me that he had a wife at home... I was more worried about his three dogs in his car!

There were moments of doubt, and times when I felt very lonely. It was sometimes not much fun being on my own, missing my soul mate and fellow Scorpion – who, I believe, for over fifty-five years *has* found me seductive and beguiling! But it was all my own choice, and I had plenty of well wishers cheering me onwards. Stick with me and let's journey forth! I can hardly believe that riding a bike the length of the UK could result in so many incidents and adventures. And remember, the scorpion trait with which I would most like to be associated is as follows: 'Scorpios are honest to a fault. They always tell the truth, no matter what!'

CHAPTER ONE

'Is that right,' asked Dave, during a coffee stop on my first outing with my local U3A cycle group,' that you're doing LEJoG and on your own?'

'Shhhhh!' I hissed, but it was too late. I felt all eyes swivel towards me. I could see the expressions of incredulity on the faces of my new acquaintances, as they turned in unison to study this newcomer to the group, who had arrived on an *electric* bike! The word was out and now there was no going back.

Most people who have an interest in cycling will know what LEJoG stands for, but for the uninitiated, it is the name of the route between Land's End, the most southerly tip of the UK, in Cornwall, to John o' Groats, situated on the extreme north-eastern tip of Scotland.

My electric bike had singled me out as different, new to the sport, and my clothing reinforced this image. Most of the ladies looked very professional in padded cycle shorts and clip in cycle shoes, riding drop handlebar bikes with very skinny saddles. But my Paramo jacket, waterproof over trousers and a pair of sturdy lace up shoes confirmed my love of mountain walking. My sit up and beg bike even had a basket in front! I am sure that I looked more like Miss Marple, equipped to do her village rounds, than a seventy-year-old grandmother intent on taking on a thousand mile trip.

You don't wake up one morning and announce 'You know what? I'm going to cycle from Land's End to John o' Groats!' So how did it happen that, approaching my seventy-first birthday, I finished my cycle ride, totally unsupported, proclaiming that, when I had finished, I felt like a seventeen-year-old again?

Come with me, whether you are making your own plans for the adventure, or reminiscing about your cycling days, and find out…

I said that I was new to the sport, but perhaps that is not entirely true. Surely most people have photographs, somewhere, of themselves on a tricycle, then a bike, perhaps leading to a motor scooter, then a car. My late father always had a bike. He needed it to cycle to and from his work, so it was perfectly natural for there to be a bike or two in the garden shed.

I was born in Glasgow and lived there until 1959 when my family 'flitted', as the Scots would say, to south Wales with Dad's transfer of work. I was then thirteen. During my childhood in Glasgow, having a bike was something which I took for granted. My memories of the freedom that I enjoyed in those halcyon days are still clear. Of course, there were far fewer cars on the roads, and children could cycle far and wide, with the biggest threat being the possibility of falling off your bike and grazing your knee. Even if cycle helmets had been a recommended piece of kit, I doubt that I would ever have possessed one. It was enough to have your jam 'pieces' (sandwiches) wrapped in the greaseproof paper that had earlier encased a sliced loaf, a bottle of water and an apple in your bike basket, your pals around you, and off you would go.

Adventures took us through the botanical gardens and out onto the Switchback, an undulating road from the north of Glasgow leading out to the foothills of the Campsie Fells, a range of hills which run along the northern side of the industrial belt in Scotland, from Stirling in the east to Milingavie (pronounced Mulguy) in the west. The open road lay ahead, and my gang of youngsters took the days as they came – so long as we were all home for dinner in the evening.

Every summer, for a month, my family rented a cottage in Lamlash on the Isle of Arran on the Firth of Clyde. It was quite a palaver getting from home on the outskirts of Glasgow to our destination. Firstly, there was a bus to catch, which took us to Glasgow Central Station, the busiest station in Scotland. There was always great excitement when we entered the huge station concourse, with trains waiting at various platforms, steam belching from their funnels. It was like entering a gigantic echoing cavern! There was so much going on to grab the attention of four young, excited children, from loudspeakers making announcements, guards blowing whistles and waving flags, carriage doors slamming shut, pigeons flying to and fro... Nowadays the din has been reduced. Modern trains run on diesel or electricity, doors close with a 'whoosh', and announcements about arrivals and departures appear silently on computer generated boards. Perhaps even the pigeons are quieter too!

We would pile into our carriage carrying our picnic, which always consisted of oatcakes, bananas and, as a holiday treat, fizzy pop. Within forty-five minutes we would arrive at Ardrossan Harbour, from where one of the Caledonian MacBrayne ferries delivered us to Lamlash, in over one and a half hours' time.

Dad would take two weeks off work to coincide with the period referred to as The Glasgow Fair. These were two weeks in the middle of July when most of the big industries on the River Clyde closed for their annual holiday. The other two weeks, when the rest of the family was on Arran, and Dad was at work, he would arrive off the ferry on a Friday night pedaling his bike. Generally he travelled with us on the first weekend so that we could settle in and collect the bikes that had been hired for us for the month. He would then travel home on the Sunday evening ferry, coming back the following Friday. At the end of the month's stay, it was left for us to pack up and catch the ferry and connecting train back to Glasgow, where Dad would be waiting on us. What could go wrong?

We were on our own in the enclosed carriage. Once you entered the carriage there was no way out, until you arrived at a station… or had to pull the emergency cord. My youngest brother was around three and had been playing with the thick leather cord which hung down on the bottom half of the door. I think it was used to pull down the window and, with the window down, you had to lean outside the train to turn the handle to open the door in order to exit the carriage. Whatever magic my brother had performed on the door I do not know, but without warning, the door flew open and wind gushed into the carriage. Ronald was miraculously captured before he was blown away, and Mum terrified us all by leaning out of the open space to try to pull the door closed. I was shrieking that we ought to stop the train, and standing astride the moquette covered banquette seats, I pulled myself up and *pulled the cord!* With a screech of brakes the train came to a sharp stop. I cannot recall the sequence of events afterwards, but the vision of Mum hanging outside the doorway trying to reach the open door has never left me.

At 432 square miles, Arran is the biggest island in the Firth of Clyde. It is known as 'Scotland in Miniature' and it is easy to see why. It is well known for its range of mountains, with Goat Fell taking pride of place at 2,866 feet. Dad soon had us walking in the mountains, singing as we went, or messing around in small boats, with no life vests! Our cycling was rather limited to the main coast road running north to Brodick or south to Whiting Bay. My least favourite holiday was our annual two weeks on the island of Millport, another of the islands to be found in the Firth of Clyde, just a ten-minute ferry crossing from Largs on the mainland. I dreaded the trip because the visit took place every 26th December and invariably the boat would pitch and roll through stormy seas in what, to a child, felt like crossing an ocean. One summer we went for our summer holiday to Millport instead of Arran. As the paddle steamer, the Waverly, approached the pier, a threatening thunderstorm broke out. Most of the passengers started to congregate on the pier side of the boat in order to get off as quickly as they could when it docked. The boat began to tilt to the one side while the paddle on the other side began to rise out of the water. My fear of unstable boats, instilled in me by December crossings, magnified, and there was no doubt in my mind that the boat was sinking! It had almost tied up at the pier, but I did not reason with that, and caused panic as I ran around the deck shouting that the boat was sinking, pleading with everyone to get in the lifeboats! Some people must have believed me, because children started to wail and there was general consternation until I was captured and subdued.

What made any trip to Millport worthwhile was that I always had a bike awaiting me, and in the two-week winter break that meant I had what I considered my own private island to cycle around. It was impossible to get lost, as a circuit of the island measured just over ten miles. From the trig point northerly views extend to Ben Lomond and the Arrocher Alps, while on clear days you can even see Northern Ireland. Millport boasts the smallest cathedral in the UK, seating just one hundred people. Seen through the eyes of a youngster I felt as though it belonged in one of Enid Blyton's adventure books. Adventures seemed magnified in the dark evenings, with the wind blowing into my face, watching the lighthouse sending out its warning flashes, and tumbling into the fish and chip shop for a takeaway or plate of mushy peas with vinegar. Dad's family had rented the same flat since he was a boy, and it had not changed since those days. The gas mantles over the fireplace hissed and spluttered continuously, the curtains flapped from the wind blowing through the cracks in the windows, and a big fire always roared in the grate. It was by the light of the gas lamps that I wrote my first story. I recall drawing lines on the paper, using my comb as a ruler. The disadvantage of this was that the comb sloped away at each edge and so my writing went uphill, along a plateau and downhill again. I sent my story to one of the Scottish Sunday newspapers. It was published and I had a postal order in return.

Reflecting upon such days, I wonder if I was such an uncontrollable child that it was easier to let me get on with things, or whether my parents were irresponsible and uncaring. I can never imagine letting my two daughters enjoy such freedom, and I almost have a heart attack when I am cycling with my eleven-year-old grandson and he tears off down steep hills at what I consider breakneck speed.

My mother died of TB when I was five. My father remarried a childhood sweetheart who had been widowed and had a son, a month younger than I. I didn't care for having this imposter thrust into my life, followed shortly by two half-brothers, so I always had a very independent spirit.

On 13th January 1959 a train puffed out of Glasgow Central Station, taking us to a new life in south Wales. It was a long, cold journey, with every click-clack of the wheels taking me further and further from everything I held dear: my friends, my islands, my mountains, my bike... I don't know why it was not part of the removal lorry's contents, but it wasn't. At school in Glasgow, we had started to learn about the works of Robert Burns, including 'My Heart is in the Highlands,' a favourite of all Scots in exile. The words echoed in my head as the train puffed onwards, and I longed to return before I had even passed the border.

At long last, we arrived in the new town of Cwmbran. Its name is derived from the Welsh *Cwm Bran*, meaning valley of the crows. There were many things I did not like. I had been used to wide roads, traditional houses, open spaces with long established parks and golf courses. Cwmbran had been built as a result of the 1946 New Towns Act. The post war Labour government had been determined to replace poor quality or bombed-out housing throughout England, Wales and Scotland, and Cwmbran was one such new town, started in 1951. New homes sprang up; new schools and shopping centres were opened. Many people, like miners from the nearby valleys, moved to Cwmbran in seek of alternative employment in the new factories and support industries. They found the modern homes a welcome change from the housing conditions they had been used to in the mining valleys.

Dad had always worked for the Royal Ordnance Factory in Glasgow, where he was an engineer/fitter. The factory was scheduled to close, and he was offered the choice of moving either to West Hartlepool or Wales. He visited the former and didn't like what he saw. That left Wales, so that is where we moved to. We left our upstairs council house, consisting of two big bedrooms, a lounge and a long, narrow kitchen, plus a shared garden where an air raid shelter was still to be found, along with apple trees and a big fruit and vegetable patch. The main living room was also the dining room and my parents' bedroom. At the end of the day a fold up bed, which fitted into the space between the chimney breast and wall, was pulled down for my parents.

Cwmbran New Town provided us with four bedrooms, albeit small in size, a lounge, a dining room, kitchen and huge storeroom. There was certainly more space for a family of six to spread themselves out. However, none of this could compensate for what I felt we had left behind in Scotland.

Within a couple of weeks of arriving, I came home from school to find a bike parked on the pavement. It had been advertised in the local newsagents and been bought for me. Thereafter I went everywhere on it. I cycled to and from school each day, delivered my newspapers on it every day…

My bike was my passport to adventure.

CHAPTER TWO

In October 1963, when cycling through Usk, a picturesque and historic town known for its salmon fishing, and the winner of the Wales in Bloom award many times, I propped up my bike against the red telephone box outside the post office and made a call which would map out my destiny.

'Yes, I'll change my mind and come to the party after all,' I told my friend.

She was pleased and said that she would introduce me to a friend named Hugh, who would be attending. 'You'll get on well,' she said. 'He's an outdoor type like you. He loves farming.'

I said that I would cycle to her home to get changed and worry about how I got home later on. Such was the confidence of being all of seventeen! Looking back, from the perspective of the modern world of the Internet and instantaneous communications, it is hard to imagine how we managed without even a land line telephone or car. Remember, we were a working class 'no frills' family, and we all cycled everywhere.

Hugh Green's parents had gone off for the

weekend and he was throwing a party. A former public school boy, he had just started his accountancy articles and drove around in his father's Humber Hawk car. In spite of our two completely different backgrounds, we had an immediate rapport. In 1968, upon qualifying, we were married.

We bought a small farm and went into sheep production. This sounds quite grand but the reality was that we owned a house and eight acres of pasture, and with wedding present money we bought twelve breeding ewes and borrowed a ram. As a town girl, I felt that I was farming Australia! Later we moved to a much bigger farm which was two miles from Hugh's practice, and so we were able to combine his work with looking after our six hundred ewes. The farming side of life was a hobby but for many farmers would have been a full-time occupation.

The years passed and cycling became something that only happened on holidays. Family photos show snaps of us with our two daughters on bikes, Helen, the younger, in the baby seat on the back of Hugh's bike. Guernsey and Jersey were favourite destinations, with their flat terrain and honesty boxes outside houses, for the purchase of fruit and vegetables. We then ventured to France, four bikes strapped onto the Land Rover. French camp sites offered everything needed to keep youngsters happy on a family holiday, from huge swimming pools, organised entertainment, lots of children with whom to make friends and perhaps the chance to start to learn another language. As we had our own bikes, we were able to explore the bays and villages around the coast of Brittany. At some time during the day we always cycled: to the beaches, to the open air markets to buy our provisions, and then one day, looking to treat ourselves,to go out for lunch...

With the aid of my school French dictionary I spent the morning rehearsing what I needed to say in order to make the reservation for the following day. We duly arrived at the appointed time to find the restaurant heaving with people and an excited babble of noise filling the air. Our allocated table was a circular one, situated in the centre of the restaurant. It was big enough to accommodate eight people, and with the distance between us and the level of noise, we had a job to speak to or hear one another. The waiter arrived, as sniffy and offhand as some French waiters can be. My choice of restaurant had not been a sound one because the menu, from the point of view of children, was very limited – from a British child's way of thinking, anyway.

'What about fish soup, Helen? Remember we watched the fishermen unloading their catches yesterday?'

'Don't like fish soup, don't they have tinned tomato soup?'

Oh dear! Suddenly I became aware of somebody kneeling between Helen and me. 'I hope you don't mind' said the newcomer. 'I could see you struggling, and you reminded me of the first time we came to France. Let me help you.' My saviour explained that most restaurants almost always offered ham or omelette with chips for children, or they would split an adult meal between them. She took control and ordered the whole menu for us, but more importantly, she told me that if we intended to visit France again I ought to go to classes to improve my rusty O level. She added that, every time we returned, I would find it easier to communicate. Oh! I wish our paths had later crossed so that I could report my progress to her.

It now seems inconceivable that once upon a time everyone benefitted from something called 'night school'. Evening classes were provided by local authorities, free of charge and through these classes you could learn a range of educational and practical subjects. Upon returning home, I enrolled for a two-year course in A level French. At that stage I never realised how useful I would find my newly acquired skill.

My love of France has never left me. I joke that there are still vibes from 'the Auld Alliance' circulating in my Scottish blood, and indeed, to visit Aubigny-sur-Nere, city of the Stewarts, in the Centre-Val de Loire region, is like visiting Scotland. Basically, the French and Scots got together many years ago and promised to stick up for their respective countries against the English. Aubigny-sur-Nere is twinned with East Lothian, Scotland. In 2015 the towns celebrated their fiftieth anniversary of alliance. In Aubigny-sur-Nere, this connection is still celebrated every Bastille Day, when Saltires, the flag of Scotland, flutter throughout the town – there is even a bag-pipe band! Charles de Gaulle described the alliance as 'the oldest alliance in the world' adding, 'In every combat where for five centuries the destiny of France was at stake, there were always men of Scotland to fight side by side with men of France, and what Frenchmen feel is that no people has ever been more generous that the Scots with your friendship.' 1995 saw remarkable celebrations marking the seven hundredth anniversary of the beginning of the alliance – not bad going!

Until my 50s, my life was devoted to my family, the farm and Hugh's practice. He had eventually set up on his own and became one of the best-known agricultural accountants in the county.

Supporting Hugh and our two daughters throughout their busy lives left no time for bikes. Instead, I was a most unenthusiastic Pony Club mum, ferrying Helen around shows and gymkhanas. Most of the mothers were reliving their youth as they encouraged their offspring over jumps, around dressage arenas, and over cross country courses. I found it all quite terrifying and boring!

Our older daughter, Jennifer, spent a few of her late teenage years in Annecy, France, and I was a regular visitor. Annecy is a beautiful town situated on a lake on the French/Swiss border. It is known as Little Venice because of the canals which flow through the old town. The lake is fed by waters pouring from the surrounding mountains and is believed to be Europe's cleanest because of strict environmental regulations introduced in the 1960s. There is an excellent cycle pathway which follows the trail of an old railway track around the thirty-mile circumference of the lake. During the day, when my daughter was working, I would make many laps around the lake on her yellow bike.

I was quite excited to discover that the route passed the village of St Jorioz. Besides being a pretty village and marina on the edge of the lake, it would probably hold little significance to the passing holidaymaker. But on my first tour of the lake, I stopped at The Hotel de la Poste and felt as though I was rubbing shoulders with history.

History has always been my subject, and I had developed an interest in the role women played in the French Resistance during WW2. I felt sure that this was the place where the SOE (Special Operations Executive) agent Odette Sansom had been betrayed and captured in 1943. Readers may recall the film *Odette*, which featured Anna Neagle and Trevor Howard. This told the story of her life, including her work as an SOE, her capture and incarceration in some of the most notorious prisons of this era in France and Germany, and her ordeal in the concentration camp of Ravensbrük.

I bravely entered the foyer and asked if my memory served me correctly. The receptionist was delighted to share her knowledge with me, even producing a box of old photographs of the hotel and its surroundings in the '40s. Nowadays a click on a mobile phone would bring up all the information I needed, but how much more satisfying it was to enter the hotel and to feel a part of the story. Good old bike! I took a photo of Jennifer's yellow bike parked at the hotel entrance, thanking it for having led me to this spot. Cycling opens doors all the time, in all sorts of places.

With our daughters starting to lead independent lives, Hugh and I eventually had more freedom to venture on holidays abroad. We headed for France more and more, encouraged by the quieter roads, better cycling weather and the French way of life. We became involved with our local Twinning Association, between Chepstow and Cormeilles in Normandy. Our hosts were a retired couple who lived in a traditional half-timbered house referred to as Colombage.

They kept some sheep on their few acres of land, but best of all was the discovery of several bikes in one of the outbuildings. The highlight of our annual visits to Cormeilles revolved around arriving to find 'our bikes' serviced and awaiting our arrival. While other members of the Twinning Association spent their break visiting touristic hot spots, we were more than happy to explore the local countryside, visiting farms and relishing the freedom which cycling afforded. Did we ever imagine that for our fiftieth wedding anniversary we would push our bikes off the ferry at Roscoff and cycle down the west coast of France to Santander in Spain? That's another story!

Our adventures in France grew and grew, with our preference being to stay for a few days in bed and breakfasts where bikes were on offer. How I dreamed of having my own bike at home so that my holiday enjoyment could become the norm. But reality always kicked in when I considered the British weather and my location in a very hilly region of Wales; how much cycling, I asked myself, would I realistically do?

Matters came to a head in 2016 when we were cycling around the Ille de Rey, a flat island off the coast of La Rochelle. It is now connected to the mainland by an impressive toll bridge, and its popularity during the summer months has earned it the name 'the new Riviera'. In late September we found the island much quieter and enjoyed days of cycling on cycle paths between the sea on one side, vineyards and villages on the other. This was as good as it got, and I resolved that for my seventieth birthday, the following month, I would have an electric bike. It needed to be an electric one if I was to get any benefit from it.

My hill-walking group had finished a hard day's walk in the Lake District, and we were sitting on an elevated hillside awaiting the bus to take us to Keswick. I saw two cyclists speeding up the hill at such a rate that I suspected they were on electric bikes. I speak of the days when these bikes were in their infancy. I approached the couple, who had rested not far from my party, and asked about the bikes. As I had hoped, they asked me if I wanted to try one out. Setting off on an electric bike is a moment that any cyclist is sure to remember. That surge when the battery, at your command, clicks into gear and you feel as though you are flying... That experience had been tucked away for another day, and that day had arrived.

As an avid reader, I always have a book or two on the go. My nose is generally stuck in books about adventures, be they about mountain walks, travel or, of course, cycling. I had devoured one such book about cycling from St. Malo in Brittany to the south of France, and thought that I might like to take this on. Why not think big and go in at the deep end? I researched electric bikes and decided that I needed something fairly solid, with tyres that were as puncture proof as possible. A good range of battery distance and waterproof panniers were also top of my list. I also had to have a step-through bike, not requiring me to throw my leg over cross bars before I got going!

So, off to Bristol I went to make my purchase. I felt very brave when I said that I intended to do longer distanced rides, but not so bold that I owned up to intending to cycle through France as my starting point! I chose a red Gepida Reptilla bike, which cost around £2500. It is a fairly solid beast, weighing in at twenty-three kg. Add on three kg for the battery, plus the weight in the panniers, you can see that I had quite a bit to control. Compare this to an average road bike weighing around 10kg.

The distinct advantage of an electric bike is that the motor helps propel you along, and cycling uphill becomes a dream. People sometimes say, 'Ah, but that's cheating!' to which I always reply, 'Yes, but you still have to pedal.' Other advantages are that cycling on an electric bike is easier on your back, neck and joints. If I ever needed proof of this, it is to compare the difference from cycling on a static bike, which I do not enjoy one bit, and leaves me with aches and pains.

My bike has eight gears and four speeds ranging from economy, tour, sport and turbo. The choice made within these ranges depends upon several factors. To make the most use of the battery, cycling in economy is, well, the most economical, best used on a level road. With a good road surface, I can bowl along in economy mode using gear five, six or seven. This, however, is quite rare, and a more average speed would be achieved in economy gear four. If I am presented with a small incline, or start to cycle into the wind, then I may increase the mode to tour or even sport. The top speed of turbo is called upon when I am presented with a steep incline, I have often wished that I had a super turbo mode at my disposal!

My bike has a monitor on the handlebar, and on this I can tell what speed I am doing, how many miles I have done, what time of day it is. It will also pick up any problems the bike has and display a warning message. I believe that I could even connect to the Internet via my iPhone, but that is getting too technical for me. My aim was to cycle as safely and to be as comfortable as possible.

The cyclist still has to put in a lot of effort, which gets one's heart rate up and blood pumping around one's body, yet the effort is a comfortable one. Often, in sunny conditions, I see my shadow keeping me company and can hardly believe that this is me, effortlessly gliding along.

The weight of the person and what is being carried on the bike will also play a part in the bike's performance, as will the weather. Cycling into a gale will sap not only the bike's battery, but the rider's too. It can take up to six hours to recharge a battery which has been completely depleted, which is why, when I had the chance to recharge en route, I always did so. It was prudent to always have my battery as fully topped up as possible. The recent increase in sales of electric bikes speaks for itself, yet there are still some in my U3A cycle group who shun them.

It felt surreal when I set off with my son-in-law, Richard, his bike carrier on the back of his car, to collect my bike! I wondered if my ambitions were really pie in the sky, and whether turning seventy had been the moment in my life when I had started to lose some of my reasoning. Now everything was up to me.

My neighbour, a keen cyclist himself, had the previous year cycled from his home in Wales to the family holiday home in Limoges, France. Not only that, his fourteen-year-old daughter had accompanied him. I had been involved with planning the expedition because Ian, his wife Annette and I met every Monday for what we called our French class. Between us we all tried to improve our French conversation, and as the person with the most experience I became involved with them making their plans. I felt part of the adventure, and the fact that Ian and Laura could cycle the distance on ordinary bikes gave me confidence to dream that their dream was mine too.

Over Christmas, Ian and I ventured out for a short ride together, and on our return my monitor indicated that we had cycled fourteen miles, including a couple of steep climbs. To me it felt as if I had just finished the Tour! Gradually my distances increased and, little by little, I began to have a sneaking suspicion that I could take on a bigger challenge. I thought that I would bond better with my bike if it had a name, so I asked my grandson if he had any ideas. Because my bike was red, Thom thought the name Piro was appropriate. He said that the name was something to do with fire. The name appealed, so I welcomed my friend Piro into my life. It is silly, I know, but it felt a lot better to have a bike with a personality and name, rather than just calling it 'bike'. Sailors name ships, so why shouldn't cyclists name their bikes?

CHAPTER THREE

There comes a time in all of our lives when we realise that our children have matured into adults and that they are starting to look after us in the way we have been used to nurturing them. My daughter, Helen, lives across the fields from our small barn conversion, and I am in touch with her most days. I had already mentioned my ambitions to her, and her response had been, 'Hang on, Mum, why not start with something more modest?'

'OK,' I replied, 'how about I cycle from home to Glasgow?' Somehow this idea grew into cycling LEJoG, with the comforting thought that, if anything went wrong, I would at least be in Britain. I had, of course, already been muttering to Hugh about having an adventure on my new bike, and in his quiet and patient manner, he let me mutter, knowing that, when I had finally decided upon what I wanted to do, he would then give me his full attention.

The year after I completed my cycle ride I was in a car park about to set off with my cycling group to do the Radnorshire Ring, a circular eighty-four mile route that embraces some challenging climbs through wild and isolated Welsh countryside. Some of the group who had raised eyebrows when they had heard about my intention to cycle LEJoG were now in awe of my achievement – so much so that Brian, unloading his bike near to where I was standing, eagerly told a passing dog walker, 'See that woman over there? She's cycled the whole length of the UK.'

To which came the uninterested response: 'Why on earth would she want to do that?' Why indeed?

The first recorded end-to-end walk of Great Britain was undertaken by brothers John and Robert Naylor in 1871. So people have been undertaking this challenge for a very long time. There are so many different routes that people can take depending upon their preferred transport: bike, horse, walking and so on. Unlike the Naylor brothers, walkers now have the advantage of many well-documented 'Ways' that link routes across the country. An acquaintance started his retirement by walking the West Coast Path as far as Bristol, continuing on Offa's Dyke Path from Chepstow to North Wales, then linking up with the Pennine Way, which took him into Scotland. By using other recognised 'Ways' he was able to get to the north of Scotland, when the distances between villages made the logistics of continuing too difficult to overcome and he abandoned his mission.

The popularity of walking LEJoG gained more

attention with the publicity given to Dr Barbara Moore's walk from John o' Groats to Land's End, which she completed in twenty-three days in the early '60s. The image of this sturdy Russian scientist flashed up on black and white television news reports, and as a schoolgirl at the time, I eagerly awaited the updates. Not that I had any aspirations to do the same thing – not then anyway – but there was something about the adventure of her walk that I found appealing. The '60s are looked upon as an era of change, be it in fashion, music or attitudes. People started to challenge and question authority, everything we had always accepted as being 'for our own good', and here Dr Barbara Moore was in a class of her own. Not only was she a vegetarian but a breatharian too. This was a word which would have been incomprehensible to most of the general public at that time. What it meant was that she believed it was possible for people to survive without food. On her walk, her diet consisted of nuts, honey, raw fruit and vegetable juice. She also claimed that, by following her diet, she had cured herself of leukaemia. She attended what is thought to be the first vegan meeting in 1944 and said that people could live to two hundred years of age by abstaining from smoking, drinking alcohol and sex! For all her theories, she died at the early age of forty-five, bankrupt and emaciated because of her refusal to eat. Each to their own!

If the nation couldn't quite find the will to fully

understand Dr Moore, I am sure it found the efforts of Ian Botham, the famous cricketer, much more to its understanding. His first walk, in 1985, from John o' Groats to Land's End, attracted much attention, raising money for Leukaemia Research. Ian had been inspired to raise funds after visiting a hospital ward where young children were being treated for this heartbreaking disease. It has been recorded that, during his first walk, the response from the public stunned him. I can echo this sentiment. My contribution to help with the fight against women's cancer pales into insignificance in comparison, with Botham having raised many millions of pounds during several long-distance walks, but the response I got from the public was much the same. I was overwhelmed by the generosity of everyone who got behind me. I am certain that, if one believed in Dr Moore's theories that fruit, nuts and vegetables could cure leukaemia, then, with the backing of the public, Ian Botham would have been able to unload tanker loads of what was needed.

When people want to raise money for worthy causes, walking or cycling the length of the UK is a popular avenue to go down... or up! On the back of this, so many businesses have sprung up, from hospitality venues en route, to firms which will deal with the fundraising and distribution of money collected, to firms offering support in helping the end-to-ender achieve their goals.

The route is also one which attracts people

aiming to break records, be it the fastest time, the oldest or youngest person to complete the distance within a certain time... The variations are as endless as the modes of transport used. Record breaking has never held any appeal to me. I cannot understand why anyone would want to cycle through all that the UK has to offer without having time to stand and stare, to absorb the tranquillity and peace the route offers. For me, it was enough to enjoy myself, and consider that every day I had broken my own personal record, achieving something which I might never have done.

I never thought of my venture as a whole, I concentrated on one day at a time. This approach made the whole project seem more manageable. When I was at the end of Mount's Bay and I looked behind me, over the water and into the distant hills of the peninsula, I could hardly believe that I had actually cycled that far. On the other hand, at times in the Highlands, I had views before me which stretched so far that they became lost in the horizon, and I found myself muttering, 'Gosh, what a long way I have got to go.' It did not seem possible to cover such vast distances, but broken down into stages, I knew that I could make it.

What about the two places that mattered most of all? The start and the finish. Land's End, as the name implies, is generally considered to be the end of mainland England, as far south as you can go before you hit water. In fact, the last land position is at the Lizard, some nine miles further south. Likewise, there is a misunderstanding about John o' Groats. It is not the most northerly point in the UK. That honour goes to Dunnet Head, which is two miles further north. The cyclist has the chance to come off the recognised road route and cycle out to the Head, in order to say that the furthest point north has been reached.

I had never considered cycling one thousand miles on my own. There would be so many obstacles to overcome that the notion was simply overwhelming. I would have had no idea about how to go about such a venture and so I decided to investigate companies that offered support services. There were several to choose from, offering programmes catering for the young and super fit, who could fly through the route in seven days, to the slower folk like myself, who preferred to take a month to complete the challenge. The advantage of doing LEJoG with a company was that I would have had back up support should I have had any problems. I knew nothing about the technicalities of a bike, not even how to fix a puncture. This way, I would have company en route, and if I felt tired, or had strained a muscle, then I could have a lift in the support van.

There were fewer firms offering support for the month-long ride, and the one I chose asked me to forward my details, including information about myself, my bike, my experience and *my age!* I was full of hope and excitement as I completed the application form. Imagine my disappointment when the secretary phoned to say that I was unsuitable to be included in their programme. She would not give the reason for my rejection. I had felt that we had developed a rapport, so much so that I had never considered there would be a question about my suitability. Was it my age, or the fact that I had an electric bike? I would never know, but as I put down the receiver, I said, 'Sod it, I'll do it myself!'

This made me wonder if I *could* do it myself. While scanning my bookshelves for inspiration, I discovered the Cicerone Guide *End to End Cycle Route*, which I had bought in 2014, with the receipt still inside. It was a volume that had niggled at me those years I hadn't had a bike. I took this discovery as a good omen and it encouraged me onwards with my planning. Cicerone Guides are simply wonderful! These books are treasured by walkers and cyclists throughout the world. In the UK these publications lead you up most of the country's serious mountains, along well-known walking trails, and on your bike you are assured guidance along some of the best known long distance routes, such as LEJoG, Coast to Coast, Peak District, and so on.

What I liked about the End-to-End guide was that it had been written by Nick Mitchell who is a veteran of numerous End-to-Ends, so he knew what he was writing about. For every route, highlights are pointed out, with the inclusion of coloured photographs to whet the cyclist's appetite for this adventure! The route is laid out in stages. At the start of each stage there are the starting and finishing points, accompanied by Ordnance Survey Map grid references, the grade of the ride is indicated, and there is information about where you can get refreshments en route. Although I never kept to the suggested daily mileage, because it was too much for me to cope with, I nevertheless found it very easy to adapt the route to my preferences.

What I especially appreciated were the maps. Opening the pages where the day's map could be found was like opening a road atlas. At a glance I could see road numbers and names of towns and villages. The cycle route stood out boldly on a bright red line, with the blue direction of travel arrow pointing in the onward direction. En route the symbol of a tankard indicated pubs and shops, and every so often the mileage between towns would be indicated. There was a profile of each day's section, where I could see how high I would need to climb, or not, indicated in both feet and metres, along with details of the towns I would pass and mileage that would be ridden in that day. At the back of the guide an appendix gave full details of bike repair shops in local towns, including telephone numbers and email addresses. What was there not to like about such a treasure trove of information? It was January 2017, and what better way to pass the dreary winter months than planning a one thousand mile cycle ride covering the length of Great Britain?

The recognised route is around nine hundred miles, but I knew that, returning to the country of my birth, I would add on visits to family, and there was the distinct possibility that I would sometimes get lost. With a little detour, I would even be able to have a night at home along the way, as the route wound its way up the Wye Valley heading for Monmouth.

Ah, but a little knowledge is a dangerous thing. Discussing the proposed route with my husband, he confirmed my anxieties about the twisty A466 leading out of Monmouth en route, and asked me if there were not quieter routes I could follow. This led me to purchase the Sustrans book, *Land's End to John o' Groats on the National Cycle Network.*

The National Cycle Network, which has its origins in Bristol, was set up in 1977. The name Sustrans comes from the words 'sustainable transport',which I think was a good choice, considering that cycling, next to walking, must be one of the most sustainable ways of getting from A to B. It has the aim of providing people with safe places to cycle. Its vision is to create a UK-wide network of safe and accessible traffic-free paths for everyone. What a commendable ambition!

Everyone should support this marvellous organisation, which has created over 12,000 miles of signed cycle routes throughout the UK, including over 5,000 miles of traffic-free paths. Money for the funding of these projects comes from various sources, supported by bands of local volunteers. One could generally say that Sustrans uses deserted railway lines, canal paths, tracks through woodlands and quiet rural roads. When planning any cycle ride, be it local or longer distance, the Sustrans web page should be one of the first to be consulted. You could lose yourself for hours or days or weeks immersed within their pages – I know that I did!

At the start of the book there is some basic information about how to get to and from the start and finish of LEJoG, some general practical information, then it is straight into the route. Because anyone following National Cycle Routes would be following route numbers instead of road numbers, at the beginning of each section there is a list of the numbers needed on the day's route, along with a map covering the whole section with towns marked and also indications where the route number changes. There is also a page giving an outline of the section and what you can expect to see and experience during it. Then there is a daily profile which mirrors that of Cicerone.

I decided to combine the routes outlined in the two books, the Sustrans and the *End to End*

Cicerone Guide, feeling that a mixture of both would suit me best. So began my planning. What fun I had, reading and re-reading what had now become my two bibles.

If this all sounds as though I am a supremely fit person chafing at the bit, ready to take on any challenges, this is far from the truth. I was encouraged by my daughter, Helen, to think about my medical history, to reflect that I had had my share of ups and downs, and perhaps my nether end might not be too comfortable being on a saddle day after day for many miles. This was true. At the age of thirty-three, pre-cancer cells in my womb led to a hysterectomy, followed in later years by a rectocele and cystocele, when the walls of my bowel and bladder, missing the support of the womb, began to cave in, requiring operations to prop them up again. Add in gall bladder removal, and spinal discs complaining about the strain of years of heavy farm work, Helen gently suggested that it might be better if I just continued to follow other peoples' adventures and not risk doing further damage to myself. I had also, in the past twenty years, suffered from a complaint called fibromyalgia.

Fibromyalgia is a condition which varies from person to person, but generally you can say that a person with 'fibro' will experience pain and general stiffness, especially in the morning. Many other symptoms can come into play, such as tiredness which can resemble the flu, poor sleep quality… the list goes on. Personally, I am affected by flare ups, which can occur for no apparent reason. It is often impossible to predict when a flare up will happen, though sensitivity to touch is my best indicator that my body is not happy. More predictable triggers are cold weather or over-stretching myself. I know that when I am in warm climates, I feel like a flower unfurling my petals to the sun, and in such conditions everything is possible.

However, LEJoG is not guaranteed to be a cycle in the sun! Books will advise you to consult the medical profession if you are about to subject your body to exercises that are out of your normal comfort zone, and I thought that, in this case, it was sound advice.

I live close to Monmouth on the Wales/England border. A search about Monmouth will reveal that it is an affluent town, with both a Waitrose and Lidl, two well established public schools, situated on the edge of the beautiful Wye Valley, an Area of Outstanding Natural Beauty. What is not reported upon is that the service patients receive from the Wye Valley Medical Practice is second-to-none. This is evidenced every Christmas, when you observe the cards and gifts that have been handed in as thank yous to all the doctors, nurses, receptionists and pharmacists who look after the health of their patients.

I have a good rapport with my GP, so I wrote to her outlining my plans and asked her what she thought about them, adding that perhaps I may need something more than paracetamol tablets to help me through one thousand miles on a bike. I expected a negative reply, reasoning that if I thought that I needed drugs to do this madness, then I should already know it was a bad idea. But when she telephoned me, I could hear the excitement in her voice! She said it was a wonderful idea, and that she would prescribe some anti-inflammatory tablets, adding that, when I had finished my ride, I would feel simply wonderful. She also gave me her telephone number and told me to contact her at any time about any medical concerns I may have. Wow! I later learned that my GP is a very active person herself and a keen cyclist too. She is often seen doing her country rounds on her mountain bike. One hurdle was over.

Years ago, in order to keep myself as fit and supple as possible, I had started pilates lessons, and for over twenty years it has played a huge part in my life. If you ask people if they know about pilates, some will ask if it's something like yoga, others will say that it's a sort of exercise, others will never have heard of it. In simple terms pilates is a physical fitness system developed in the early twentieth century by Joseph Pilates, after whom it was named. It is a form of exercise which concentrates on strengthening the body through the core strength of your muscles, leading to an improvement in fitness, flexibility, balance and wellbeing. The exercises are done slowly, with control, often using a soft ball, called a chi ball. I have been fortunate to have had many years of instruction from a first-rate instructor. At the end of lessons, even after so many years, I have to tell her that she makes every lesson unique and that, through pilates, I am still learning about my body and how to care for it.

In preparation for my ride, I had some private lessons with Jennifer, my teacher, where we concentrated on the muscles that would play a vital part in my trip. I was asked to attend the leisure centre with my bike, laden as it would be when I undertook the journey. To begin, I cycled around the car park, where Jennifer could observe my seat on the saddle, the relation of my legs to the pedals and so on. Straight away she noticed that my one knee was turning in towards the bike, when the correct position is that both legs and knees should be parallel. Some lads were cycling past and I could see that the turning in of knees was a common thing for many people on bikes. On a short run this would not result in any problems, but having a bad posture for over one thousand miles of pedaling would start to put your body out of alignment.

I started to work daily on exercises to strengthen my quads, to keep my hips open, my neck relaxed, my spine supple and so on.

Throughout my trip I was religious about doing my pilates exercise every morning and evening, and there is no doubt that this contributed to my success. Since finishing my ride I have given talks to local groups, and I have often been asked if I could give an example of a useful exercise. There is one exercise which everybody could easily incorporate into daily life, and that is to pay attention when looking left or right, when at a road junction in your car, for example. How easy it is to just turn your neck, but if you can think about your nose, and let your nose lead you around your shoulder, your eyes will follow much more smoothly and much further. This is just one small example of how pilates can help you to use your body with kindness and efficiency.

The lesson had gone well, and I was aware of the weight I was carrying in my two panniers. We progressed to the lane outside. It was pouring with rain, and I cycled along avoiding the potholes. But when I started to turn around to cycle back to where Jennifer was waiting, disaster! I failed to see a big pothole covered with leaves, and as I turned the wheel, it dropped into the hole, jammed, and I felt myself tilting off the bike. It was like a slow-motion film, and there was nothing I could do to break the backward fall. I landed with a thud on the road. The back of my head took the impact to the extent that my crash hat was split down the middle. Luckily, because of the design of the helmet, which took the brunt of my fall, my back did not suffer and neither did any other part of my body. I was pretty shaken up, all the same. This was a valuable lesson about paying attention to road surfaces and always to expect the unexpected.

I was to think about this upset throughout the miles which followed. I was also becoming acutely aware of other pitfalls. In bright conditions, the boughs and leaves of trees cast shadows across country lanes; this can be disconcerting to the rider as the road surface appears to dance all over the place, and as such it is impossible to tell if there is a rough surface ahead. When passing houses, I was on the look-out for children and dogs running into my path. Meanwhile, a discarded bottle or piece of rubbish could also spell disaster if it became tangled in the wheel. I never wanted to fall off my bike again.

My plans were still under wraps, and I was unsure whether I dared announce my intentions. The next step was to have a word at my local leisure centre to investigate proper training in the gym. I knew the staff behind the desk as I have gone there for over twenty years, every Wednesday for pilates' classes, in addition to the odd swim in the superb pool.

The first time that I confessed my plans, I approached the desk and uttered the words, 'I am planning to cycle from Land's End to John o' Groats. What must I do to get fit for this?' I expected sceptical replies but instead I was taken very seriously and was told: 'You must speak to Adrian, he did it years ago.' So I booked an appointment with Ade, one of the instructors. He listened to what I had to say, as I expressed both my intentions but also my fears. Then I was put through a series of tests, to assess my levels of fitness. One test was to pedal a static bike. I had to pedal and pedal, and weights were added as I did so. Of course, the task became harder as the weights were added, but this didn't bother me much, and I was happy to continue. At the end of the time trial, I was told 'Well done, you have the engine inside you of someone half your age!' Ade enthused how a female in her thirties would have had a job to keep the pedals turning as I had. He offered help and advice, saying that, with training, I would be up to the task, although he was the first to caution me that the first three stages from Land's End would be the toughest.

We agreed on a training plan. I duly arrived at the centre the following week, for my one and only experience of training in the gym. I hated it! Even pedaling on the static bike didn't feel comfortable, and I could not see the point of training on all the other complicated bits of equipment. I mentioned this to Ian, the manager, on the way out. He told me not to worry and said that it was all about the bike, to keep cycling and that fitness would come. He was correct. He then suggested that perhaps I ought to have a few swimming lessons in order to increase my stamina, and I readily agreed.

I was introduced to Dawn, the instructor, and this meant that I had to let her into my secret too. She too was full of encouragement and we set up a training programme. The first time that I emerged from the changing room wearing my goggles, my swimming cap and nose clip (I had yet to perfect breathing under water without one) I jokingly said to Dawn that I felt as if I was about to swim the English Channel, to which she replied, 'You can come with me next month when I will be swimming it for the fourth time.' I reasoned if she could do that, surely I could cycle one thousand miles.

So began our training, throughout which I learned a lot about muscles, how they function and the benefits of training in water, which lends its support to the body. Soon I was walking up and down the pool, frontwards, backwards, sideways, marching up and down, swimming with flippers, swimming relaxed style. Dawn was certainly the best teacher I could have had, and week by week I could feel my fitness improving.

I was on track with my training programme and things were beginning to fall into place. Maybe I could do this after all?

CHAPTER FOUR

I had been researching cycle equipment and was soon cycling with padded shorts and proper cycling gloves, which helped with the vibration from the handlebars shuddering up my arms. But I still preferred my lace up shoes to the clip on ones favoured by the experienced cyclists!

I had progressed with the planning of my route and started to seek the advice of a few trusted friends. I have a neighbour, Phil, who has competed in many serious cycling challenges, and even builds his own bikes. I took him into my confidence and asked if he thought I was mad. In an email he replied 'you set an interesting challenge'. He elaborated that, on LEJoG, keeping to forty miles a day, even on an electric bike, was no mean feat. Again, I was told about the challenges of the first three days of the ride, and Phil gave advice about a training programme on my bike. He suggested that I ride three consecutive days a week. The distance was not important, but undertaking such a training schedule would help me to identify any points of discomfort. Apparently, what stops many people are problems with their feet, knees, bottom, neck, hands and arms. Such niggles often lead to cyclists jacking in the whole thing. To this end, he advised me to make sure my saddle was set at the correct level. This sounded very much in line with what Jennifer had been advising me.

By March I reported to Phil that I had booked accommodation as far as Bristol, that my route planning was coming on, but that I kept dithering and changing my mind as I assessed and re-assessed routes. I voiced my concerns about cycling through bigger towns. It seemed to me that I was finding more obstacles than I had imagined, but I never lost my conviction that this was something I felt that I could achieve. I wanted to do it!

Everything was taking a long time, especially as I was combining two routes. On my computer I have an Ordnance Survey map of the UK, which I used a lot in my hill walking days. I turned to this to plot my routes and work out accurate mileage for each day and get a fuller feel for the topography. Although there were profiles given in each of the books, I developed a more substantial feel for the journey as I plotted my route within the bigger picture of the map. By March I had decided upon my final plan, which would take me around thirty-three days, including three days of rest. I will expand upon this as you journey with me through the stages.

Next, I began booking accommodation. Where

possible I booked through Bookings.com. This had the advantage of, in general, not requiring a deposit to be paid in order to secure the booking, as well as offering the right to cancel should I not be able to honour the booking because of breakdown or injury. Hugh said that he would never want to do business with me and questioned how anyone could run a business with such generous terms!

On all my reservations I explained what I was doing and asked for confirmation that I could park my bike, securely, overnight. Piro spent overnights in locations ranging from my bedroom to beer cellars, garden sheds, back gardens, garages, laundries... Most people were generous in accommodating my needs. Not so Mrs X in the wilds of the Forest of Bowland, from whom I had a terse reply telling me that my fifty percent deposit was non-refundable and that she expected full payment a month before my arrival. Hold on! Mrs X also ran a campsite, and these were the terms relating to that side of her business, and not those laid out relating to a one night stay in her hotel, as advertised on Bookings. I contacted Bookings and explained what had happened. They took control, took Mrs X to task, refunded my deposit and all was well. Well, not quite, because Mrs X then wanted to charge me for her time in having to sort out this misunderstanding! In fairness to Bookings, I was asked if I had any expenses I would like to claim and, yes, I did.

My research suggested that bookings in remote villages in the Highlands of Scotland should be made well ahead of time, as the scarce accommodation was often booked up months in advance. Hence, February found me having a conversation with Mandy, who originated from Merthyr Tydfil, a town not so far from where I live. I made my reservation for a date in July, and her only condition was that, if I was not going to turn up, could I please let her know. She went on to explain that she often had stranded cyclists arriving at her home and had even put people up on her lounge floor. With no single bedrooms available, I readily offered to share my twin room with any females who may be seeking a bed for the night. Asked about a deposit I was told not to worry, to cycle safely, and just to keep in touch. What a difference in attitudes!

March was upon me, and my training reverted to cycling the ten-mile round trip between our two farms, where, every spring, I help my husband with his hobby of lambing his sixty ewes, which he combined with his everyday job, from which he took a few weeks off. Some years ago, I fell into the habit of going to Mallorca every April, on my own, for a week of relaxation to get over the work involved with lambing what was then six hundred ewes. I joined walking groups in the north of the island, mixing my days in the mountains with days on the beach. But recently I had taken up painting and started to visit an artist who ran painting holidays on the island.

Ralph Hedley, a well-known international artist, has lived in Mallorca for many years. He now runs a business under the name of Paint Mallorca. Thanks to the miracle of the Internet I came across his tuition course. I liked his style of his painting, so I took a deep breath and signed up to one of his courses. As luck would have it, I was the only person who had applied for my chosen week, but Ralph decided to continue all the same. The first time I flew to Palma I was met by Ralph's wife, Tina. We are the same age, and we immediately hit it off. I had no idea that I was rubbing shoulders with such a famous person! Tina (Rainsford), Ralph's German wife, has had a spectacular singing career, especially in Germany, where she is a star to this day.

I was driven to the beautiful farmhouse where she and Ralph live, in Santa Margalida. In spite of all my reservations about my poor painting abilities (particularly as I was now to receive one to one tuition) I was made so welcome and soon felt quite at home. From that day on, this delightful spot has been a wonderful springtime bolt hole for me.

But in April 2017, I decided that, instead of having painting tuition, this year I would spend my time cycling. Ralph and Tina confirmed that, in Alcudia, a seaside town a few miles from their home, I could hire an electric bike – great! I wanted to follow the professional cyclists who spend the winter and spring in the northern part of the island.

Mallorca has, for many years, been a Mecca for cyclists, with its warm and predictable weather, range of terrain, and smooth roads. Most of the cyclists who visit the island tend to base themselves in the north east corner, in the towns of Alcudia and Port de Pollenca. At one time the type of tourist attracted to these towns wanted to drink and party all night, giving the British holidaymaker a bad name, but now the area is geared up for cyclists. These days, cycling is reckoned to be worth around €150 million euros to the local economy. In the spring months, the roads in this part of the island are packed with teams out training.

There always seems to be a cycle competition taking place. On one occasion I was cycling past a village when I heard the wailing of a siren coming towards me. I immediately thought that there was an emergency ambulance or police car approaching. I had no sooner pulled into the side of the road than a peloton of around three hundred cyclists whizzed by, with a police escort!

I had confidence that if I could cycle, daily, for a whole week with no repercussions, then that would be the confirmation I needed that I could cope with LEJoG. My friends took me to the cycle shop, where Ralph explained, in Spanish, what type of bike I needed. He was the first person I heard proclaim, 'This lady is going to cycle from Land's

End to John o' Groats, the whole length of the UK!' It was very strange for me to hear this; it sounded so serious! I cannot imagine that it meant anything at all to the shop assistant, but she made appropriately encouraging remarks.

My hired bike was similar to Piro, and I immediately felt comfortable with it. Ralph and Tina drove home while I found a waterfront tapas bar and spent a leisurely hour familiarising myself with my cycle maps and contemplating the week ahead.

It was a true *Shirley Valentine* moment, as I gazed over the azure sea and soaked up the sun. Unlike Shirley, in Willy Russell's play and later film, my life was anything but in a rut; and unlike Shirley I was, already, missing Hugh; but with the warmth enveloping me, the sun bursting out of a clear blue sky, and the smell and atmosphere of foreign surroundings around me, I too felt a rush of self-assurance. *I could do this,* I thought. Just like Ralph had said: I was going to cycle the whole length of the UK.

It would have been easy to forget about training and to slip into holiday mode, but any such temptations were soon dispelled as I mounted my bike, which I named Amigo, and pedalled off to join the throng of holiday makers and serious cyclists. Wide cycle lanes are found at the side of most main roads in Mallorca, and I never felt at risk, even cycling on the opposite side of the road to that which I am used to.

With my local map, I set off every morning, cycling forty to fifty miles each day. I had no trouble locating stops for a coffee, rows of parked bikes indicating the trusted watering holes of the cycling fraternity. Sometimes my route took me close to beaches, and I was able to incorporate some sunbathing and a swim. I couldn't help but thank my lucky stars for my freedom and health, which allowed me, in the category of old aged pensioner, to be able to do what I was doing, not forgetting the finances to support such adventures.

A sign had been posted outside Ralph's finca saying that the side road would be closed on Sunday between noon and six in the evening, owing to a cycle competition. That morning, I set off on my daily ride, completely forgetting about this warning. As I came through Santa Margalida at 4.00pm, I could see that the square was full of cyclists involved in the race.

Dash it, I thought. *I wonder if I will be able to get through*. I knew of a shortcut off the main road, and if I cycled along this track, I would arrive at the entrance to where I was staying. Surely this would not interrupt the race? The cyclists were leaving the village at half hourly intervals so there would be a free moment or two when the road would be empty.

I managed to cycle along the track, but when I came to the road I needed to cross, I was met with a very stern official who directed a volley of words at me, in Spanish, of course. I thought that I would try the innocent holidaymaker abroad approach and mimed that I didn't understand Spanish. Unfortunately, my guard spoke perfect English and left me in do doubt that, although I pointed to my house opposite, I could not gain access and would have to wait for two hours until the road opened. Like a dog with its tail between its legs, I turned around and cycled back to the main road again.

Then I had a cunning plan... Blend in with the crowd! When the next lot of competitors had left the official starting point, I joined them at the back of the peloton, and to all intents I was part of the team. Oh! The joy of passing my official and giving her a cheery wave as I swept into the driveway of where I was staying!

At the end of my week away I had cycled the equivalent of Land's End to Bristol. As I sat on the plane watching the shores of Mallorca recede below me, I gave myself a mental pat on the back. I really could do it!

Back home, word of my trip soon started to leak out, and I was asked what charity I was supporting. I had never given this a thought; wasn't one thousand miles a big enough challenge, let alone raising money? However, I slowly came to realise what an opportunity my trip presented. But what charity would I choose? A trawl through various websites left me more confused than ever. Every single one was a deserving cause! I was drawn to anything that supported blind children, because I had once worked with a colleague whose child had been born blind, and even to this day I think about that child. I cannot imagine a life without sight.

In the end, though, I decided upon a charity called Women V Cancer. I was initially drawn to it because of the logo, which is of a woman on a pink bike. The charity represents the three women's cancers – breast, ovarian and cervical – and raises funds through the sponsorship of many numbers of women cycling in groups; every year there are thousands who cycle from London to Paris. You have to pay a registration fee and pledge to raise a minimum amount. For this you get support en route, your ferry fare is paid, accommodation, meals, etc. are organised, and perhaps best of all, you are part of a huge crowd, supporting each other the whole way.

The charity also organises LEJoG rides. I reckoned that, in every town I would pass through, a woman and her family would be facing cancer in some form, be it diagnosis, treatment or recovery. And here was I, aged seventy, my health enabling me to undertake such an adventure. If my bike ride could, in any small way, aid funds to fight women's cancers, then that seemed like a good choice.

I contacted the charity to ask if I could represent them, but on my own. They had never heard of anyone doing so but were pleased to give any support they could. The charity started to send me t-shirts and trinkets to hand out, but I did not need nor want any of this. All I wanted was their approval to use their logo and to be associated with them. I said that I was organising and paying for the whole venture myself.

The paying part was easier than the organising part. Others cycle LEJoG and en route stay in youth hostels or camp sites, as they count their expenses. I understand this; I had calculated that I would need to spend around £3,000 in accommodation and daily expenses alone, and I appreciate that such a budget is not within everybody's remit. However, I knew that for the venture to be a success then I would need to take care of myself, having a good night's sleep, eating properly, and receiving body massages wherever possible. I had enjoyed my days of youth hostelling, not least the priceless experience of Black Sail Path, but now was the time for some comfort.

Plans were taking shape, but I needed help with the practicalities of promoting my venture and coping with modern technology. Luckily, the staff of my husband's company, Green and Co, Accountants, came to my rescue. I was allocated a member of staff, Michael, to whom I could turn for advice, and without his support my ride would have passed unnoticed.

Firstly, Michael laminated a map of the UK showing my cycle route from Land's End to John o' Groats, and these were put on the spine ends of my panniers. Then he laminated two large Women V Cancer logos which I affixed to the sides. People passing by could, at a glance, see what I was doing and why. I then had cards produced, headed with the pink Women V Cancer logo and giving details of my website. When people donated cash, which was mostly the case, I gave out a card and encouraged donors to look on my webpage later on. Every night I recorded donations on my blog so that people could see that their money really was going to my charity.

I set my target at £500, reckoning that the odd person may toss in a pound or so. I never imagined that I would collect over £7,000. The generosity of people is one of my overwhelming memories of my experience. When I was training locally and people started to learn about my adventure, they immediately rose to support me. I never asked for donations or tried in any way to promote myself, but from the moment my site opened there was not a day went by that donations were not made. I was flabbergasted to see that donors were pitching in £100 online, but it was the sentiment behind the donations that humbled me most. One morning the local refuse van passed me, and straight away the driver and his assistant handed over £5 each. I knew that they probably didn't earn a huge wage, and I will always remember their gesture. Some people choose to donate anonymously, but the person who holds the Just Giving Account can always see 'in the background' the name of the donor. There was a comment by an anonymous donor, that a £20 note had been found when walking along a tow path. I was intrigued to discover who this could be, and I saw the name of a local family that had already given a generous donation. Upon my return I mentioned this to Emily and she told me that it was the money that her twin daughters had found. They had decided to donate to my cause. I might have expected teenagers to think 'finders keepers' and find something on which to spend their newfound gains – but no, they decided that it should go elsewhere. I was later able to thank them, much to their embarrassment. What lovely girls indeed.

Amongst my final preparations, I made a couple of very simple and effective contributions to my success, one low tech, one high tech.

Firstly, the low tech: I had a two-pronged device fitted to the back of Piro, on which I flew the Scottish and Welsh flags. I was afraid that drivers could become inured to cyclists on busy roads, and I felt that, with my flags fluttering behind me, I was sure to catch their attention. I did not realise what an important part these flags would play in my travels, both during LEJoG and on subsequent rides through France, Switzerland and Spain. They were always a big talking point. I had a mirror mounted offside my right-hand handlebar, so that I had clear vision of vehicles coming from behind, and, with these simple devices and my bright clothing, I felt that I had done everything possible to cycle safely.

The high tech: I was given an Apple iPhone! My daughter reported that the salespeople in her company would be updating their phones, and this meant that I would have the chance to buy one cheaper than the normal cost. When her boss heard why I needed a phone, he kindly said there would be no charge. My old PAYG phone, on which £5 would last me a year, was suddenly redundant. I now had to learn how to use this new piece of equipment, and, to my amazement, I was soon using it to keep my own blog!

I quite enjoyed becoming a blogger. When happily pedaling away, throughout my day, I would be thinking about what I would say in my daily report, and what photos I would upload. I developed a rhythm of posting around 7.00pm, which, as someone told me, put me up against *The Archers*: the serial about British farming which is so loved by so many. What competition!

With help, I could download my route to my phone, and I would be able to Google my position en route; I would never be lost... Well, in theory. I had a tracker on the phone so that my family would always know exactly where I was. I found this magical. I joke that I am still in the age of the quill pen, and this is not far from the truth. My preferred method of corresponding is writing with my fountain pen on quality notepaper. This, I know, is very outdated, and people may mutter about the waste of paper, etc., but that's how it is.

My preparations were over, and I was soon packing my two panniers with my gear. I had chosen two Outeredge panniers, made in a sturdy, box-like design, fully waterproof, with a zipped section on the front, they were easily clipped onto the back rack and had good rubber handles to carry them by hand. One was marked 'kit', and consisted of the following:

Full length cycle trousers
¾ length cycle trousers
Cycle shorts
Walking shorts
Waterproof over trousers
Waterproof jacket
Waterproof hat for over helmet
Waterproof cycle cape
Waterproof over shoes
Two cycle tops, cycle vest
Neck muffler, which doubled as a
head scarf for under   my helmet.
Berghaus Primaloft jacket
Windproof yellow cycle top
Lace up shoes
Cycle gloves, short and full fingered
Sports bra
Socks
Crash helmet

Then there was my personal pannier, which consisted of:

Underwear
Nightdress
Crushproof trousers
¾ length trousers
Blouse x 2
Sweater
Lightweight casual shoes
Toiletries
Handkerchiefs
Hair tongs

My tongs may seem like a luxury, but to me were a necessity! In one flap I stored my iPad and my very special, bright yellow leather purse, which had two zips on each side, for a total of four pockets. I had marked each section 'keys and paperwork', 'phone', 'cash', and 'bike monitor' respectively, so that at a glance I could see exactly what I needed to put my hands on. Joining my bag were little extras, such as bike rag, oil, plus my list of accommodation throughout. I know that everything can be downloaded on to phones, but I preferred the old-fashioned comfort of having written confirmation. My notebook, my cycle books, the cards to give to those who had donated money, battery charger… It all added to my luggage.

Piro was almost ready for me. I know nothing about the mechanics of electric bikes, and so before departure I took out a breakdown policy with ETA Cycle Insurance, for a very modest cost, hoping that I would never need to use it. In front of my handlebars, I sported a small bobbin-style wicker basket in which I always had water available, there being no realistic way to incorporate water bottles on the frame. I now realise how very amateurish this was. I later moved onto a Click Fix waterproof bag, which was much more practical and efficient.

On 2nd June Hugh took me to Land's End. How strange it felt to be loading up my bike and gear, realising that all my months of preparation were about to be put to the test. I felt ready, physically, emotionally, practically and just wanted to get on with the job. I worried about lots of things: about breaking down in a remote spot, injuries, meeting unsavoury men on lonely lanes... But hang on a minute, I was a seventy-year-old gran, who was going to have designs on me?

It was sunny and very windy, late afternoon, when we pulled up at the Land's End car park. The car park attendant said that, as a LEJoGer, I didn't need to pay the parking fee. We wandered around the resort, which was closing down for the night, but I was able to sign my name in the official book, in readiness for my departure the following day. Gosh, this was getting serious! There was also time to have a quick whiz around the small museum, where we enjoyed reading the stories of many people who had, in their various ways, travelled from Land's End to John o' Groats. My endeavours would never compete with their achievements, but I would be doing it my way, with no back up support. Any problems would be my problems. It all rested with me.

Over the years, many lesser-known people have made the journey, on many varying forms of transport. The appeal of travelling the route seemed to know no bounds! I was later told about one person who had pushed his way north on his scooter, ending up with one leg twice the size of the other!

Our first night's chosen accommodation was at St Just, a few miles from Land's End. I rated Wintera B&B as one of the best in which I stayed throughout my trip. It was a benchmark, and the breakfast was truly superb. It offered everything one could wish for and set me up for my first day on the road. The charming owners said that I was the first LEJoGer on an electric bike that they had hosted, and also the first on a bike with a basket in front. It looked as if I had set a record before I had even begun! They made a donation towards my charity, something I was to get used along my travels. Then there was nothing else for it. It was time to start my adventure!

CHAPTER FIVE

Day One, Saturday 3rd June
Land's End to Perranwell: 40 miles

By 8.30 on a bright, breezy morning, I had unloaded the bike from the car, hooked on my panniers and edged up to the starting line. It being early in the morning, there were few people around, so I was surprised when a young woman ran towards to me, almost hugged me and wished me well. She recounted that, years ago, before she was married and had had her family, she too had cycled LEJoG. 'I would love to come with you, I envy you!' she declared. What a wonderful start!

Her young son looked up and asked, seriously, 'Are you leaving your man?'

'Yes,' I replied, 'but not for always.'

With loud cheers ringing in my ears, I left 'my man' and my fans, all clapping and waving me off as I rolled down the narrow path leading out of the car park. I was heading for Perranwell, a distance of forty miles away.

It was always my preference to stay in country inns, where I could eat in the evenings, and to avoid big towns and main roads whenever possible. However, before I could follow my chosen route, I had to cycle a very short way on the A30. As I pedalled up a short incline 'my man' was waiting for me at a bus stop pull in bay, just to check that I was OK. What a lovely surprise, especially after our emotional goodbye just a short time before.

Hugh left for home to get ready for shearing, and I cycled off reciting Burns' 'Ae Fond Kiss, and Then We Sever', sincerely hoping it would not continue as the ballad does: 'Ae Fareweel, alas, For Ever!' Our brief encounter cheered me as my journey proper now commenced. I was full of confidence, but I knew that Hugh was full of concern.

Sustrans advises quitting the car park and heading for Sennen Cove, to the north, on route 3, also known as the Cornish Way. The route then loops around, crosses the A30 and continues on route 3 towards Penzance. The End to End route follows the A30 directly to Penzance before linking in with route 3, which sweeps around Mount's Bay. My preference was to leave the A30 as soon as I could and wiggle down through the country lanes leading to Penzance.

I had read that route 3 suffers from sand being blown onto the track, making cycling hard work, and because of this I decided to set out on the A30, which, as it turned out, had very little traffic at such an early hour. It was easy to follow the roads outlined in the books, leading me towards Mousehole and Penzance at a steady pace. As my trip progressed, I found myself slightly altering my organised routes more and more.

Many tales of cycling exploits recall cyclists camping where they fall down, letting their adventure unfold as it happens, with no thought about where they will sleep until they reach a village and hope there will be some type of accommodation. Not only would I have not enjoyed this, 'my man' insisted that every night I was somewhere safe and that someone was expecting my arrival. He telephoned every morning and evening and worried about me throughout the day.

He needn't have worried. I was in my element cycling around the quiet lanes. Road surfaces were generally good, and the odours of farming accompanied me, with cow pats on the lanes and wildflowers dancing in the wind on roadside verges. It was a pleasant surprise to meander through country lanes and see family farms engaged in traditional farming. I felt that I had taken a step back in time, to a truly rural environment of yesteryear.

At Mousehole I was able to glide into the village overlooking the harbour without any restrictions. Freedom was mine. I had no car to park, and I could cycle wherever I chose.

Both routes meet at Penzance, where they follow

Sustrans route 3 for the four-mile traffic free zone that follows the bay to Marazion. The whole way St Michael's Mount was in sight, sitting resplendent on its island below me.

Upon recommendation, I stopped at Philps' Bakery just outside Marazion and bought a wonderful Cornish pasty, which was so big that it also served as lunch the following day. Here, I met my first fellow cyclists, also stocking up. The comparison between us was stark. They were a group of three young, strong lads planning to do the trip in around a week, whereas I resembled the tortoise, on my own, taking my time. They wished me well and were the first of many to say how much they admired my courage to be cycling alone and with no back up.

Soon the two recognised routes parted, the leisurely one heading north to St Ives Bay, while I stuck with the smaller lanes heading east, which would lead me to my first night's accommodation, at the Norway Inn, Perranwell. Although my books warned of the first stage being hard and tiring, I found my first forty miles had presented no real challenge. Had I continued for the whole of the recommended stage of sixty-five miles, perhaps I would have felt differently, but I arrived at my destination at 3.30pm and congratulated myself on a good day.

I was warmly welcomed by a young Australian girl who was working her way around the world.

She was a wonderful young hostess, first helping me up the twisty stairs with my panniers, then leading me to where Piro would spend the night in the outhouse. I knew she would go far in life, with her open and helpful attitude, and I enjoyed a brief chat listening to her aspirations. I felt tired, but a lovely bath soothed my aching limbs, followed by pilates, sorting out kit and so on, in preparation for the next morning. It was no more than a few steps down to the bar for some pub grub and a catch up with the newspaper. I had resolved to stay away from alcohol in case it should impair my performance, and though this pledge did not last, this first evening I felt a mixture of sadness and virtuousness as I kidded myself that at least the local water was very good!

Day Two, Sunday 4th June
Perranwell to Fowey: 30 miles

The E-E book stated that this stage would be tiring, and today I was to appreciate the truth of this. I arrived at Fowey with only one bar showing on my battery and was so pleased that I had stopped overnight where I had. My blog for the day recorded that the 'thirty miles were steep and challenging but my training at home had stood me in good stead'.

My route took me over the King Harry Ferry, a chain ferry which transports people, bikes and up to thirty-four cars across the river Fal. I lined up with the others awaiting the arrival of the ferry. It was Sunday morning and some people looked very elegant in their smart cars, out for an enjoyable day trip. I stood out in my cycle kit, a lone cyclist resting over my handlebars. During the brief crossing, I was approached by a couple in a vintage Morris Minor car who told me that they were motoring LEJoG later in the year. I wished them well, and they gave a generous donation.

My next challenge was St Austell, the first town of any size that I had to negotiate. It being a Sunday, the roads were relatively quiet, and with cycle slipways next to most of the main roads, the End to End route led me easily around the edge of the town. My book advised me that I could digress to visit Kilmarth, the home associated with the author Daphne du Maurier, but my anxiety about my battery meant that I continued directly to my destination.

The timing of my arrival could not have been worse. I arrived at 1.00pm, bang on lunchtime, to find the King of Prussia Hotel on the quayside absolutely heaving both inside and out. It seemed that the whole world was drinking, smoking and eating. I pondered what to do. It did not seem like a good moment to interrupt the hard-working staff, although I was within my time of check in. Asking someone to keep an eye on Piro, I fought my way through to reception to suss things out. Full marks go to the staff of this wonderful establishment.

Straight away one of the assistants took me across the lane to the cellars, where I could safely park Piro. She then helped me to carry my luggage to my room on the top floor overlooking the quay.

I had opted for a superior room and was so glad of this decision. I was never again going to repeat this journey, so why shut myself away in a back room when there was the opportunity of a room with a window on the world outside? And what a view my widow gave me! My diary records that 'my room is excellent [underlined] in every way, with White Stuff toiletries, being bright and clean with a sitting area overlooking the noisy square. Ear plugs are provided, plus bottled water and fresh milk for the tea and coffee facilities.'

I enjoyed my cup of tea as I surveyed the heaving crowds below. An artist was doing a roaring trade sketching portraits, but with my developing artist's eye, I rather smugly recorded that I didn't think much of his work!

It was a perfect summer's afternoon, so I set off to explore, walking up to the headland and the coastal footpath. En route I met an elderly gentleman who was folding up his electric bike, waiting to be collected by his wife in her car. He enthused that, with his advancing years and living as he did in a hilly area, investing in an electric bike was one of the best things he had ever done. We spent a few moments discussing bikes, with my new acquaintance happy to tell me about his exploits in his younger days. 'Wish I was coming with you, lass. Good luck! Here, put this towards your charity.' Men always seemed to have a five or ten pound note to hand!

My walking tour took me around the many little shops, but I was not tempted by anything as I did not want to carry extra weight – though I did find room for a tea towel with a picture of my hotel on it. A plaque on the edge of the quay commemorated the site from which ammunition was loaded for the US army division that landed in Normandy on D Day, 6th June 1944.

Returning to my lovely room, I decided that my evening blog could wait. The Internet was poor, and by evening most of the day trippers had left, so I could go down to the much quieter restaurant and enjoy a good meal, before getting my head down for an early start in the morning. A gale was forecast for the next day, picking up strength throughout the morning.

Day 3, Monday 5th June
Fowey to Torpoint: 30 miles.

What a contrast in two days! With just a coffee, toast and a banana for breakfast, I was heading out through the twisty, narrow streets in full wet gear, as the wind blew and the rain started to spit down. I carried a bacon and egg butty and a coffee, which I knew I would appreciate later on. At the Bodinnick Ferry, which would take me across the river Fowey, I got talking to a big group of cyclists who were doing LEJoG as part of a package. One of the leaders came over and told me that I would eat into my battery this day. How right he was! Immediately after my leaving the ferry a very steep hill awaited, and even with my battery to help me, I found it a struggle. Without an electric bike it would have been impossible for me to have even thought about taking on such a torturous route. I resembled a flying red Batman as my cape flapped behind me, but I was still snug and dry under my waterproof clothes. Although I had my route downloaded to my phone, I felt no need to consult it as I found the directions in the Cicerone E-E book faultless. I dropped off at Looe to enjoy a hot snack in a café, with Piro looking very forlorn outside as the rain set in.

All the same I determined to digress and visit the seaside resort of Downderry. My late in laws had honeymooned there and had been so taken with the place they had named their house 'Downderry' after it. I was curious to see what the attraction had been. Perhaps in the 1930s it was the place to honeymoon, but I could find no charm that would have lured me there.

But perhaps others could say the same about my own honeymoon in 1968, when we crossed the relatively new Severn Bridge for a one night stay in the Cotswolds. We returned the following day to our smallholding, where we got stuck into mucking out the calves' sheds. This done, we picked blackberries that we sold to a local fruit shop the following day en route to work. For our labours we were paid one shilling and four pence a pound. There was no such thing in those days as a honeymoon in an exotic country. Work was always the order of the day, and nothing much has changed, with Hugh at seventy-six still working pretty much full time.

I passed a cemetery where I noticed headstones indicating the graves of servicemen from World War Two. I realised that it was the eve of D-Day, and that weather conditions had been much the same in 1944, very unseasonable and stormy.

I was becoming concerned at the rate at which the bars on my battery were falling as the demanding hills gobbled up the electricity. The last thing I wanted was to run out of power on the windswept cliffs. My Cicerone book warned that 'the next eight miles from Plymouth involved some of the most challenging traffic conditions in the whole E-E route'. I took this very seriously, and it worried me so much that, in the end, I decided to take the Sustrans route 27, known as the Drake's Trail, which would take me from Plymouth to Yelverton and on to Dartmoor. However, that was for tomorrow and I first had to recover from today.

I limped into Torpoint at 1.30pm, having been cycling on one bar for some time, expecting at any time Piro to tell me that I had better start to pedal my heavy load myself. The pub I had booked had sounded very good, with good reviews, but unfortunately, I got off to a very bad start. I knew that the pub was ordinarily open from noon, so even if my room was not ready, I could shed my soaking clothes and get out of the pouring rain. Ah, but I had overlooked that it was Monday, which meant the doors would not open until 3.00pm. I thought about moving on, even to dreaded Plymouth, but with no battery left, I had no option but to wait. When I was ringing the bell, to no avail, another guest came along. He too was trying to get inside and had the number of the owners. I did too, but in my frozen and desolate state this fact had not registered with me.

When the owner eventually appeared, he was in a grumpy mood and reluctantly admitted me, but said the chap would need to come back later on. I was not sure if he thought my new acquaintance might creep down from his room and drink the bar dry, or if he took pity on me, but whatever the case, I was the chosen one! The chap didn't mind, as he had his car and said he would go and get something to eat.

My booking had confirmed that there would be an indoor slot for Piro, but I was told that this was no longer the case and it would need to stay outside. There were loads of nooks and crannies where Piro could have been parked up, and on such a wet and miserable Monday evening there were very few customers to inconvenience, but I had to accept what I was told.

My room was just about acceptable but was so cold. I was wet through and shivering, but I was told that the heating would not come on until later in the evening and 'didn't I know it was summer?' I didn't feel at all welcome, and I am sure Piro felt the same. As the afternoon wore on and I snuggled in bed to try to get warm, I was glad of my bacon butty from my breakfast, but longed for something hot or even a brandy to warm me up

This experience of poor hospitality was the worst I experienced during my month away. Elsewhere, if I had had bad weather, hosts bent over backwards to do whatever they could for me and my bike. Here, there was nothing for it other than to stick it out, and as the palm trees outside were bent almost horizontal in the gale, while the wind threw the rain into the windows with such force that I feared the panes might break, I took some comfort that I was not cycling in it. It was a good job that I didn't know what Scotland had in store!

Day 4, Tuesday 6th June
Torpoint to Mortonhampstead: 45 miles

I was glad to leave my accommodation, and before long my mood was lifted by the warmth of strangers. Before I got onto the Torpoint Ferry, which would take me across to Plymouth, I stopped at a bike shop, where my tyres were checked and my mirror, which had begun to wobble, was fixed at no cost.

On the short crossing, which is free for cyclists, I got talking to a group of bikers my age, waiting alongside their motorbikes. Looking at them in their outfits, I wondered if they were the mods and rockers of the '60s, still living it up. They certainly stood out in their leather gear, some of it studded, some of the men wearing their hair tied back in ponytails. In normal circumstances our paths would never have crossed, but here we were, people of the road exchanging our news. They were keen to tell me of the parts of the UK that they had been to on their bikes, and said they would never consider exploring other than on their motor bikes. I had the impression that they did not know whether to pity me or to admire me.

Very soon the ramp was down and I was pedaling off the ferry, as they roared by with a cheery wave. I always find that there is something exciting about getting on and off ferries. The crossing itself, be it long or short, marks the end of one section of a trip and the start of another, with a new horizon at the end of the ramp. In this case my new horizon led me up a fairly steep incline, towards traffic lights. This was where I would leave the E-E route as it followed the busy roads around Plymouth. I now had to find Sustrans route 27, which I had incorporated into my itinerary. As I was pondering my direction, a young lad, on his bike on his way to school, crossed at the traffic lights and approached me. He took in my panniers and I will never forget his words: 'Cor, mrs! Are you going all the way to the north of Scotland on that?'

I replied that yes, that was the plan. He said he had no money to give me, but offered me the remains of the packet of biscuits he was munching! He said that I would need them more than him, but I assured him that I would be fine! He told me that he would think about me, so I gave him my card and said he could follow my nightly blog. Whether he did or not I will never know, but perhaps, one day, he may recall the old lady he met who was cycling to Scotland and undertake the ride himself.

I eventually found my way to my route, having sought help from dog walkers on the way. On both occasions I was given donations. Seeing my flags and logos people were generally very interested in talking to me, wanting to tell me about their visits to Wales or Scotland. 'Why have you got both flags?' I was often asked. I explained that my husband was Welsh and I Scottish, and so the flags represented our respective countries.

It was still blustery but dry and bright, and I was thrilled to find the Drake's Trail had a good tarmac surface. But my euphoria was short-lived. The route was strewn with debris from the previous night's storm, which made progress slow. Then, to my great horror, Piro began to miss beats as the electricity cut out. I groaned and pleaded with my bike not to give up on me in this isolated spot. I thought that the battery was probably wet from the overnight stay out in the pouring rain, so I took out the battery and dried off the points, clicked it into place, and set off again. It was a case of stop and start all the way to Yelverton, where I linked with the E-E route on the B3212, which would take me over Dartmoor. I had a lunchtime stop at a pub in order to recharge my battery, but it didn't make any difference. Whenever I asked if I could recharge my battery I would offer to pay for the cost of the electricity, but it was always given freely, so a good tip was called for.

My afternoon continued in the same vein: a sudden, short burst of energy followed by no connection. I had to pedal without assistance. This was very hard, tiring and dispiriting work. My climb over Princetown and Postbridge meant a steady, determined push on the pedals. 'Keep going, keep at it,' I encouraged myself, as Piro and I made slow progress towards the summit of 1,400 feet. The challenge seemed endless and I was becoming very, very tired.

Squally showers were the order of the day. I sheltered in the lea of any trees I could find on the roadside, and little by little the wind helped blow me over the moors, passing en route the famous prison and medieval clapper bridge at Postbridge.

My book mentioned that a visit to the prison museum was well worthwhile, and in normal circumstances this would have been right up my street, but right now all I could think about were the hills that stretched upwards and onwards before me. Likewise, I had to forego stopping at the solid yet simply constructed clapper bridge, which dates from the Middle Ages. These types of bridges were constructed so that pack animals and people could cross the many rivers and streams found throughout Dartmoor. The bridge, which I would cycle past, is considered as one of the best preserved in the region, but that too would have to wait for another day.

Arriving at Mortonhampstead at 4.30pm, after an 8.30 am start, I felt like I had had a very long day indeed. My back was complaining, my whole body was sore, and it was time to try out some of my GP's magic pills. My B&B host at the Old Post Office was welcoming and used to hosting cyclists. He was concerned not only about me, cycling on my own, but also my bike. However, he confessed that I was his first guest on an electric bike, so unfortunately he was unable to help me. It was comforting, all the same, to have such a sympathetic host.

The Internet connection was, once more, poor, but over a very good evening meal in a bistro in the village, I began to feel restored. I caught up with Helen, who rang to say that Thom's school was following me and wondered if, when I had my day off at the end of the West Country stage, I would call at his school with Piro, for the boys to ask me questions. I readily agreed.

Before I fell into a deep sleep, I prayed that tomorrow would be a better day.

Day 5, Wednesday 7th June
Mortonhampstead to Corfe: 46 miles.

Miracles! I awoke to a fresh, sunny day and Piro was on best behaviour. The traumas of yesterday receded as I tackled my next challenge of navigating through Exeter. I got a little lost, but with the good cycle tracks in the city, my delay was minimal. I was just happy to be cycling normally once again.

But my joy was short-lived. After thirty-three miles, in the village of Talaton, Piro died on me once more, my monitor showing the message 'error 503'. I knew that I was in serious trouble. I needed help, but the phone connection was so poor I decided to freewheel as far as I could towards a main road, where I hoped the signal would be better. But before too long I had to implement plan B. I needed help right now!

I stopped on a triangle of grass at a road junction in the deepest countryside. Huge tractors were going to and fro with their loads of silage. It was a chaotic situation in which to find myself. I made contact with my ETA Cycle Insurance and asked for assistance. I was asked for my post code, but I had no idea of what this might be. I offered an Ordinance Survey map reference but that was no good, so I said that I would have a breather and phone back when I had the information. In the meantime, I would try to reach the A373 leading to Honiton.

I started to flag down cars, asking for the local post code, but they were few and far between and no one that did stop could help me. It was later on that I realised that, had I been more efficient with my new mobile phone, I could probably have sorted this out myself! A gentleman stopped his car to ask if I needed help. He was so concerned for my welfare that he offered to stay with me until help arrived. When I assured him that I would be fine, he gave me his card, with all his details, and offered to put me up for the night. Who said I wouldn't be accosted by strange men!?

I arranged with my insurance company that I would get to the village of Payhembury, where I would be collected and taken to a bike shop in Taunton. I had also been in touch with the shop in Bristol from where I had bought Piro, and they gave me the good news that I had broken down in the very best part of the country. In Taunton there was a company which was the headquarters of the import and distribution of my make of bike. I contacted them and explained about the warning message, and I was assured that this was an easy problem to sort out. They would expect me at 9 the next morning. Things were looking up!

As I waited in the village, passers-by became involved in my drama, and a lady insisted that I push my bike around to the local garage to see if Steve could help me. He Googled my problem and declared that I had a problem with the sensor, but said I would need a specialist shop to get it sorted and reset. Nevertheless, I was comforted and impressed by all the strangers who were willing to give me their time, in simple acts of kindness to help someone in trouble.

My taxi arrived. It was of a special design which enabled Piro to be wheeled into it. Before long we were delivered to our sumptuous B&B, Wellies, in the charming village of Corfe. I had phoned ahead to say that I would be arriving later than expected, and was welcomed to my tastefully furnished room with a cream tea waiting for me. Oh! I was ready to do justice to the delicious scones, jam and cream, washed down with a couple of cups of tea. Arriving at this haven of tranquillity after such a stressful day was just the panacea I needed!

Day 6, Thursday 8th June
(Corfe) Taunton to Priddy (Wells): 42 miles

The following morning, my driver arrived promptly, to take Piro and me to Nationwide Electric Bikes in Taunton. I didn't expect to be delayed long, as I had been assured that my error would be simple to rectify, and I still held hopes of completing my sixty miles to Bristol.

I arrived at the cycle shop, where the door was held open for me with the words 'Come in, we are expecting you.' Darryl, the mechanic, set to work immediately, but alas, my troubles were far greater than had been envisaged. Darryl spoke to Bosch in Germany about an apparent problem with the motor, the upshot of which was that he took a motor out of another Gepida bike to replace mine. 'Good,' I thought, 'I'll soon be on my way.'

But my twenty-eight-inch wheel needed the motor of a corresponding bike, not the twenty-sixth-inch wheel bike out of which Darryl had initially taken the Bosch motor. All this mechanical work took time, and as the hours ticked away, I patiently waited, counting my lucky stars that I had broken down in such a fortunate spot. Had my misadventure happened anywhere else, then my trip would have been over. Nationwide saved the day, and I never once felt from them anything less than a genuine ethos of care and interest in their customer. They replaced my mirror with a much better one, giving me a clearer view of traffic behind, and the company and staff both contributed to my charity and followed me throughout the rest of my journey. Although Taunton is over an hour's journey from my home, I continue to take Piro there for services, and when, the following year, Hugh bought an electric bike, there was never a discussion about where we should go to buy one.

It was 2.00pm before I was on the Bridgewater canal path, Sustrans Route 3, which, as luck would have it, ran just five minutes away from the bike shop. Karen, the secretary, cycled with me to point me in the right direction, then I was off, pedaling as fast as I could along flat but sometimes muddy canal paths. It had been my intention to follow the E-E route until it married with the Sustrans route at West Harptree, just south of the Chew Valley Lake, outside Bristol. However, with my diversion to Taunton, I decided to continue with route 3.

I was never going to make it to Bristol, so I contacted Hugh and asked him to collect me from outside Wells. It was Thursday, and Mrs May's general election day, though I can't say I saw any polling activity in the towns I passed through. I was tired, and another stressful day was taking its toll. I got lost in Wells, then my battery gave out, and I had no option but to pedal until I reached my meeting point at the Hunter's Moon, near Priddy, north of Wells.

While I awaited my rescue, Helen phoned, full of support and comforting words, wondering if I was still up for visiting the school the following day. What was to have been my day of rest, on Saturday, would now see me making up time, cycling from the Hunter's Moon to the Severn Bridge.

Collecting my bike in Alcudia, Mallorca. Ready to start some serious training.

Nearly ready for the off. With grandson Thom who was a regular companion during training.

Start. Looking a bit apprehensive.

Beautiful Sunday afternoon. The estuary at Fowey.

The Bodinnick Ferry. Dressed for the very wet and windy day which was forecast.

A challenging few hours going over Dartmoor. My battery was misbehaving and a lot of pedal power, with no assistance, was needed.

Nationwide E Bikes Taunton. Brilliant mechanic, Darryl and equally super manager, Karen. Without their intervention my whole trip would have ended before it had hardly begun.

Seven Bridge. Start of next stage. My supporters, brother Ronald, myself, sister-in-law Lesley, neighbours: Laura, Ian, daughter Helen and grandson Thom.

If you are lost, ask a policeman, and even if they are on a murder investigation. Note the blue gloves. They will always help!

My reluctance to cycle along canal paths. Some of which can be very narrow.

My knight on a skinny saddle. Paul, from Warrington Cycle Club who led me to Langho.
Without his help, guiding me through many towns, I would never have coped.

*Leaving Slaidburn on a very hot afternoon. The road appeared
to go on,and on, and up and up!*

Scotland welcomed me!

Sombre moments at Lockerbie.

Aunt Margaret and Uncle Mark. Still nifty at ninety.

Gathering of the Clan. Night out in Glasgow.

"Come, let me show you my bus". At exhibition staged by Glasgow Vintage Vehicle Trust, on banks of River Clyde.

With Trish and dog at the Dog Café at Bowling Harbour.
I am terrified of dogs, what am I doing here?

Falls of Dochart, Killin. Looking spectacular after heavy rain.

Cadha Mor viewpoint. Magnificent scenery.

Crask Inn. Lots of Highland cattle wandering about.

Reflections on Loch Naver.

Torrisdale Bay. On the home run!

*Reunited! I had only been expecting to see Hugh. With Helen, Hugh,
Thom and friend John Walker holding banner.*

Was I glad to see the Freelander arrive with the bike rack on the back! In spite of what had been a few emotionally challenging days, I comforted myself with the thought that it had been good to get any glitches out of the way early on, and I was confident that all would now flow smoothly. That evening, I recorded that I was thrilled with my new mirror, and that I must take more care when negotiating bigger towns, which, on the whole, were well supplied with cycle routes. I also recorded that I was 'quite exhausted'. It was bliss to be back home and in my own comfy bed!

Day 7, Friday 9th June
Thom's School

I took Piro to Monmouth, where I had been invited to join the staff of Thom's school for lunch and to take questions from the boys. I was very impressed with the interest the boys showed in the bike and my journey. They asked questions I would never have thought about! Thom's year said that they would follow my progress, and I said that I would keep them up-to-date by sending postcards from places of interest en route. Thus my trip became part of their History and Geography lessons. I decided to award a trophy that would be presented every Speech Day to a boy who had, during the year, done something of special interest or overcome particular difficulties. I imagined the award being for a young lad who had shown a bit of 'true grit', but it eventually morphed into the Geography Cup. A night at the local pub with our family and friends wound up a perfect day before I was once more back in the saddle.

Day 8, Saturday 10ᵗʰ June
Priddy to Chepstow: 42 miles

Leaving the Hunter's Moon, I set off for the forty-three miles to Bristol. Initially my son-in-law, Gary, who is a keen cyclist and lives in Bristol, had offered to escort me through the city. With my unhappiness about cycling on busy streets, I was grateful to have someone to show me the way. However, our plan fell apart with my detour back home, my planned Friday becoming Saturday, so I turned to my trusty E-E guide to take me via Long Ashton and down the gorge towards Avonmouth. I was comfortable with this because I would be in familiar surroundings. Well, familiar in the sense that it was the way of a car journey to Bristol Airport!

My route took me through Ashton Court, a country estate on the edge of Bristol. Since 1979 it has hosted the Bristol International Balloon Festival, attracting crowds of over one hundred thousand on each of the four days of the event. As it was Saturday, the park was mostly occupied by families enjoying the wide-open spaces on the edge of the city. After exiting the grounds, I arrived at a busy road junction and again had to consult my map. Bristol appeared to be in chaos because a new rail link was being constructed through the heart of the city. The route that I wanted was barred, and the signposts were covered in graffiti.

In my moment of desperation, a lady cyclist stopped and offered me help. She was out shopping and went out of her way to lead me to the start of the Portway, en route telling me interesting historical facts about the areas we cycled through. This act of kindness was something I was to experience more and more on my travels. I was never alone; there was always someone close at hand to help out. On my ride through the South West Peninsula, if I was overtaken by cyclists who saw my panniers, they would often slow down, check if I was OK and ask to cycle some of the road with me. There is definitely such a thing as a cycling camaraderie.

Once on the Portway, it was a straightforward run to the industrial area of Avonmouth, and before I knew it, I was crossing the Severn Bridge, heading up the Wye Valley road to Chepstow Racecourse, where Hugh would be waiting for me. I now had two hundred and seventy miles under my belt. I would pick up my route the following day when, supported by my peloton of family, I would cycle to Gloucester. Thereon I would be on my own.

*

Day 9, Sunday 11th June
Severn Bridge to Gloucester: 36 miles

I was now firmly adhering to the Sustrans route as it followed the River Severn northwards to Nantwich. At the start of the cycle track on the Severn Bridge, I met my brother and sister-in-law riding borrowed bikes. They had determined to see me off, even if that simply meant cycling across the bridge and back. My neighbours Ian and Laura, daughter Helen and eight-year-old Thom completed my supporting fan club. Richard, my son-in-law, drove his car in case Thom should tire. Hugh had to demur on the cycle, needing to attend to the farming work, so it was another farewell until John o' Groats before the rest of us set off.

It was a lovely sixteen-mile Sunday ride through the quiet lanes leading to Berkeley, where we stopped for lunch. Then it was time for another parting as Helen, Richard and Thom headed for home, Thom protesting that he wanted to carry on and come with me! Perhaps one day he too will cycle LEJoG, and in my rocking chair, I will follow from a distance.

Ian and Laura came with me to Gloucester, where I was staying the night. En route we met up with cyclists from the Stroud Valley Cycle Club, who led us through the edge of Gloucester to my accommodation. With an evening to myself I was able to catch up with emails and donations, write my blog, and get myself ready for the next day.

Day 10, Monday 12ᵗʰ June
Gloucester to Droitwich: 50 miles

There was a sense of adventure as I awoke. From now on I was really on my own, yet I had the comfort of still being amongst familiar landscapes. I loaded my panniers and set off for Gloucester. My NCN route would take me around Gloucester Docks, but I was familiar with the town and was comfortable in making my way directly to route 45 on the west side of the city.

As I was making my way to Maisemore I passed a couple who had, independently, cycled LEJoG by two different routes. We exchanged notes, and upon hearing my age, the chap said he was definitely going to get his mum an electric bike for Christmas! They took my card, and later that evening I found lots more donations and words of support from total strangers. My new acquaintances had spread the word on social media, and in the cycling fraternity the wheels turn very quickly. As a person who does not engage with social media, I found it amazing that people would be sufficiently interested in me to make financial donations. Perhaps my nature as a 'canny Scot' held me back from being more generous myself!

On I went along the narrow track, but before long my way was blocked by a large fallen tree. There was no way around this obstacle. I had the choice of returning to my starting point and taking the road, or doing what others had done and clambering up the bank, breaking through the hedge at the top and emerging onto the A417. I chose the latter. Unhooking my panniers, I hauled them up the bank before scrambling back down to pull Piro up to join them. There was a lot more traffic on the road than I had anticipated. Motorists were unprepared to see a cyclist emerge from the undergrowth with her bike, so I quickly hooked on my gear and was gone!

After Maisemore I had the distinct feeling of being in a different part of the country. Ordinary-looking houses gave way to traditional Herefordshire black and white half-timbered ones. Yet, at the same time I could see the Black Mountains of Wales in the distance, a reminder that I was still not so far from home. It was great to be back on country lanes once more. I inhaled the smells of freshly cut privet hedges and newly mown lawns. Peace and quiet were mine, and all felt well with the world as Piro glided northwards.

I stopped for coffee at a lovely pub at Kinnersey and asked if I was allowed to eat my breakfast, which I had brought with me. Jody was very helpful and obliging. In the morning I liked to be on the road after a coffee and light bite, stopping a couple of hours later for a rest and something more to eat, and the best way to achieve this was to carry some fruit and toast from the breakfast table, with the host's permission of course. Some people can tuck into a full English first thing in the morning, but that is not compatible with my body clock.

As I sat outside, enjoying my break and studying my route, an elderly gentleman out walking his dog ambled over to chat. 'I wish I had your pair of lungs!' he said, and then happily, albeit with a tinge of regret, reminisced about his cycling adventures in bygone years. How good it felt to be a cyclist, cycling one thousand miles, we agreed.

In Worcester I again lost my way. Then again, they say you are only lost if you don't know where you are, and I knew that I was in Worcester, trying to find my way to the Worcester and Birmingham canal on route 45; it was how to do so that was the problem! Another 'they say' is that if you are lost, you should seek help from a policeman. And who should be heading towards me but multiple policemen, wearing blue gloves and beating the grass in the parkland alongside me? They all looked quite serious, and I hesitated to interrupt them, but as we grew parallel, their eyes glanced in my direction, and I was emboldened to ask the way to the canal. With that, five of them ambled over to the fence to enquire about me. They told me that they were on a potential murder investigation, hence the blue gloves, but they still had time to chat, and we had our photo taken together.

Soon I was on the canal bank, talking to two of the lockkeepers, who advised me against the route as the paths were muddy. I asked the men if I could take their photo, but they replied that they weren't supposed to do so. However, they must have been feeling bold as they gave me their permission anyway. I promised not to post the photo on social media – as if I would have known how to!

I don't like canal paths at the best of times, as I am aware of the outcome should I veer too close to the edge of the path, lose my balance on a stone, or skid on a muddy surface. I admire cyclists who effortlessly duck under canal bridges and continue cycling on without changing their speed. My cautious nature, or fear, sees me dismounting and pushing my bike under every bridge. Perhaps it's not a bad caution. I was reminded of a cycle ride along the Brecon Canal when one of the cyclists hit his head on the bridge and ended up in the canal. Mind you, he was over six foot, but nevertheless it was an anxious few moments as he and his bike were rescued. Luckily, this stretch of canal was short, so I made the most of it and before long I was in Droitwich.

I was finding that I was reliant on my mobile phone to find my accommodation when I arrived in a town, and my arrival at Droitwich was no exception. I got the phone from my yellow purse but left my purse lying on the back of my pannier. I only discovered this when I arrived at my hotel and was aghast at the implications of having lost it. I put it down to being tired after fifty miles and made a mental note to be more careful. I had worked out that the stage would be forty miles... Oops! What with the blocked paths and muddy canal paths, I wondered if the E-E route would have been better and noted that I was starting to feel more comfortable on busier roads.

I was staying at a small hotel and my room provided a bath – lovely! After my meal in the restaurant, I was ready for an early night. I had a happy message from Helen to say that Thom had done a PowerPoint presentation at school about his sixteen-mile ride, which had encompassed his ride across the Severn Bridge. Whoever suggested I would be lonely on my travels?

Day 11, Tuesday 13th June
Droitwich to Ironbridge: 44 miles
The day started off as one of the dullest and coldest thus far. Starting and leaving a route, in most instances, is the trickiest part of a journey, so I was chuffed that my navigation aid on my phone got me from my hotel to Sustrans route 45. Thereafter I was confident that I would have no trouble in merrily following its directions to my evening's stop at Ironbridge. At one stage the route crossed the River Stour before briefly joining the Staffordshire and Worcester Canal. Once again I met two lockkeepers who advised against going anywhere near the canal paths, which they said were very muddy. They seemed to know that the whole of route 54 northwards, the Staffordshire and

Worcester canal, was in a pretty bad state and advised me to stick to roads. However, my route continued on route 45, and in no time I was at my halfway stop of the day.

My overwhelming memory of this day centres around my lunch stop at a riverside cafe in Bewdley. It was very busy. The weather had improved and there were lots of families enjoying the riverside setting. A young disabled girl in a wheelchair kept on wailing, and there seemed to be nothing her parents could do to calm her. Other youngsters, who were too young to have appropriate manners, thought this sounded like fun and started to imitate her, until I was surrounded by what sounded like a pack of baying wolves. The father was at his wit's end and eventually moved on. During this desperate situation I could not help, once again, to reflect upon my own fortunate situation. How, I pondered, would I have managed if I had had to bring up a child with such a disability? *With great difficulty*, I answered myself. The donations and messages which popped up on my page every evening extolled my bravery, my guts and determination, but there was no doubt in my mind to whom they should have been directed. That day I witnessed raw love, guts and determination, managing a situation which would not end after a bike ride but continue as a life-long challenge.

After this brief hiatus I continued on the road to

Bridgenorth and Telford. I kept seeing signs indicating route 45, but as I wasn't finding the roads very busy, I stuck to my plan and only picked up the route in time for it to lead me directly to my lodgings. The final section was heavily wooded and steep, with twigs all over the place, making cycling challenging. That evening, I recorded that I did not care for the Sustrans routes, and I wondered if I would have been better to stick, throughout, to the Cicerone Guide E-E. I was gaining confidence in my abilities and becoming more competent on busier roads, so what had hitherto seemed too big of a challenge was becoming much less frightening.

I had a warm welcome from James, my host at Calcutts House, and a fish supper in a nearby pub rounded off what had felt like another long day. I was looking forward to the following evening's stop, because I had the treat of staying at the Rookery Hall Hotel and Spa, where I had booked a massage.

Day 12, Wednesday 14th June
Ironbridge to Nantwich: 48 miles

I was now 'off piste'. I put my confidence in my iPhone and newly downloaded route. I had lost my phone holder, which had sat on my handlebars, so I tucked the phone into my bra. I gradually became irritated by the American voice drawling in my ears. Once it had directed me to 'take the motorway' I was not amused! When I wanted to confirm my route, I found that, in the bright sunlight, it was impossible to see the screen. This found me scrambling under trees and bushes as I shielded against the sun. I must have looked like a suspicious character! A passing motorist gave me advice on my route, but the truth of the matter was that I was soon lost.

Passing some houses, I saw a couple who were tending their garden. I asked for assistance and they willingly produced their map and set me on my way again. My priority was now to get my own map. I know that the younger generation can travel the world with just an iPhone, and my guides did provide detailed maps, but oh, I so longed to have the clarity of being able to see a fuller picture. This would help with my sense of direction, if nothing else. Soon I was at a petrol station, where a helpful gentleman saw me checking my tyre pressure and came to help. At the petrol station I was able to buy a *Road Atlas of Great Britain*. This was extra weight to carry, but I later extracted the relevant pages covering the whole of my journey and felt much happier to be back in control. I thought all was going well until I saw a sign for 'Newcastle'. Had my wanderings really taken me across the spine of England? Luckily, I could confer with my new map, which confirmed that the sign was for Newcastle under Lyme!

Before I knew it, I was coasting into the pretty market town of Audlem, which was bedecked with flags. The town seemed to beckon me to stop and enjoy what it had to offer, but as ever I had too many others things going on in my mind. I had need of Audlem Cycle Sports shop in the main street. There, Tim replaced my lost pump and punctured water bottle, fixed my pannier, which had lost one of its catches, had a quick look over Piro and wished me well. Despite my entreaties, he did not accept payment, so I donated to my charity instead.

While I was there, Tim took a call from a member of his cycle club and exchanged remarks about their forthcoming cycle ride. For a moment I felt that perhaps it would have been more fun to have had company on my ride, but hey ho, I had promised myself a glass of wine that evening.

My day ended on busy roads close to the Nantwich bypass. I had a rule that when I was at a T junction and needed to cross a road, I always had my gear in turbo two. This meant that I had a speedy take off, so if traffic was approaching, I could zip out of harm's way.

The sweeping driveway to Rookery Hall welcomed me. As a single person I always had to pay the rate of a double room, which at £120 for B&B was at the top end of my budget. However, as I wheeled Piro into my elegantly appointed room, I reckoned it was money well spent. I was surprised that I was allowed to take my bike into my room, as the carpet was certainly not used to having dirty tyres pushed over it! And the bliss of a good body massage is something every End to Ender should indulge in en route.

Rookery Hall was built in 1816 by a proprietor of some standing in the community, who owned hundreds of acres of farmland locally and also a sugar plantation in Jamaica. I wondered if this luxurious place had been built off of the proceeds of slavery and found it a bit disconcerting that I might be wallowing in comfort at the expense of bygone slaves. I tried not to dwell upon this, having no idea if it was true, but determined to enjoy my meal and my glass of wine in the restaurant, which boasted four red stars.

I had nobody to chat with over dinner, so my mind played back over my day in the saddle. I had chosen quieter roads, which had taken me past the famous Harper Adams Agricultural College outside Newport. I was in prime Shropshire countryside, and I could appreciate the quality of the crops of broad beans, peas, potatoes and barley. I had been wrapped up in the sounds of birds singing, the smell of mown fields and hedges. I had been at peace with myself. This was a change from my Google app chattering away; this was what cycling ought to be like: taking the slow route as the day unfolded.

The caption of the photo posted on my blog that evening read: 'After stressing about modern technology note the new addition to my gear!' The photo is of my bike, the pannier and my new road map alongside!

Returning to my lovely room I found a message from my pilates teacher reminding me of the benefits of sleep and imploring me to be kind to myself when I could. I needed no reminding, as my massage and wine rendered me ready for bed by 9.00pm. I had a sound sleep till seven the next morning!

Day 13, Thursday 15th June
Nantwich to Warburton: 30 miles

I had appreciated my little treat the day before and had planned a shorter mileage for today; I was now heading for the part of the route which, in the planning stages, had given me the biggest headache. My Sustrans route wanted to lead me through Manchester – help! The directions looked pretty straightforward, but how I worried about getting lost in a city I didn't know. I got contact details from local cycle clubs and phoned a couple of people to ask if anyone could help me. Alas, everyone was very busy – or perhaps confused to have such a timid old lady on the phone asking for help!

I had more luck when I contacted the Warrington Cycle Club and spoke to Paul, the secretary. I had got his number from my cycle magazine, and he could not have been more helpful. I decided to head north from Nantwich (there is also a Southwich, Eastwich and Middlewich) to Runcorn, where I would meet the E-E route going on to the Forest of Bowland. I had booked an overnight stay at the Black Swan near Warburton, where Paul promised to meet me the following morning and lead me to my next destination at Langho, near Whalley. In this way I would have guidance through the towns of Leigh, Bolton, Blackburn and their conurbations, which seemed to meld into one mass of urbanisation. I visualised myself taking days to navigate what looked like a complicated and busy route and thanked my lucky stars I had found a saviour to help me.

I was now entering the North West of the Sustrans route: 235 miles to Carlisle via the Lake District. I started by obediently following route 151 out of Nantwich but very soon adapted to following the B5074 road heading more directly to Winsford. The Sustrans routes tend to be more picturesque and quieter. One can appreciate the rural aspects of the journey. On the other hand, by taking more conventional roads, I was able to meet far more people. Contact with others definitely enhanced the experience, and this in particular was a day that will always stay with me.

It was bright and sunny, and I was enjoying cycling through the level lanes of the Cheshire Plain in every respect but one. Was this the area where famous footballers had their mansions? If so, they were welcome to them! The peace of rural England was shattered by the continual drone of air traffic flying in and out of Manchester airport. Where were my chirping birds?

I gave my designated route a go, but with my new map I soon adapted my own. It took me past a Premier Inn, where I stopped for a coffee. Just at that moment, a lady whose name I soon discovered to be Jo was leaving the gym. Spotting my logo, she approached me with her tales of having cycled the Rhine and the Scottish 500. She lamented that her friend, who was to start chemo for ovarian cancer the following day, had left the gym ahead of her; Jo was sure she would have loved to meet me. I handed Jo my card and said that her friend, Caroline, would be able to follow my progress. That evening I had a message from Caroline along with a donation. Here is what she said: 'Hi, Christine, I'm Jo's friend, Caroline, with ovarian cancer, op last week, biopsy results Monday then chemo plan! You are an amazing lady, thank you. I will be following you all the way.' I replied that it was she who was amazing not I. It was the first time that I had brought home to me the significance of my fundraising efforts.

My route afforded easy cycling through villages of red-bricked houses, some small cottage types, others grand and imposing. Passing one such house I spied an impressive tree house in a beautiful garden. Hugh and I had been discussing building a tree house for Thom, and I thought that this one looked just the ticket; perhaps if I had a photograph we could copy the design. I didn't want to be intrusive and thought that I had better knock and ask for permission to snap a photo. It was a gated property, so I rang the bell. Hey presto! The gates swung open and I pushed my bike through the deep, crunchy pebble driveway. A few seconds later a smart sports car swung in behind me, the driver clearly amazed to find this intruder on her property! It appeared that the driver had pressed her gate control button from her car at the same time as I was hoping someone in the house would acknowledge my call. I assumed that the gates had opened at my request, but no, it was at the driver's request, and I was simply a few steps ahead! I quickly explained who I was and said that all I wanted was permission to take the photograph.

On reflection, this could well have seemed like the latest scam of how to burgle a property, but my new friend, Sheila from Ireland, welcomed me with the offer of a cup of tea, explaining that she was in a rush to attend her grand-daughter's sports day. I was told to make myself at home and take as many photos as I wanted, and she produced a tray of beautifully laid out china and biscuits. I wondered if I had discovered a worthwhile ploy for a daily cuppa en route!

Sheila was interested in my venture, saying that she had never done LEJoG but recommending La

Manche to La Med (the English Channel to the Mediterranean), which she had cycled in her youth. I responded that this was the ride that had got me interested in buying an electric bike in the first place. I added that her ride was on my to do list. I must have passed any scrutiny, not that I for one moment felt that I was being questioned, because, before Sheila left, she told me to take as long as I wanted, to enjoy the garden and to leave by the side entrance. What a perfect hostess! Was it Irish hospitality that led her to being so kind and welcoming? How many other people would have left me to myself in such an obviously prosperous property?

As I wandered the grounds, I eyed up even more flashy cars parked in open garages, children's toys, gardening tools, pieces of equipment lying around... Perhaps living in the country as I do, I am hyper aware of the thieving that goes on. In spite of the best security measures, theft in the countryside is still a major problem. They say that in rural areas you either know who someone is or you wonder who they are. I could have been a spy for the local burglar's association posing as an innocent old dear on a bike!

After my rest, I continued on my way, the pedals turning automatically. Soon I needed to relieve myself of the copious amount of tea I had drunk, so finding a quiet field, I parked Piro outside and climbed over the gate. As I was having my wee behind the hedge, a group of cyclists rode past and I heard one shout, 'There's an End to Ender!' I hoped he was referring to my route, which could be seen on my panniers, and not me squatting in the field! With an early arrival at the Black Swan I had time to catch up on my paperwork and raise my target to £5,000. Donations were pouring in, exceeding my expectations.

I needed to be up early the following morning to welcome my escort, Paul. And before that, I had to do justice to my evening meal: a juicy steak and a glass of red wine. This wine drinking was becoming a habit! At the adjoining table four gentlemen were having a business meeting. The conversation moved fluently between French and English. I was able to follow their plans for the company, criticism of the staff and their marketing problems. I thought to myself, *Hey, besides becoming a burglar, I could become quite a little spy if I put my mind to it!* It had been a different type of day, and an enjoyable and relaxed one at that. I was getting so much out of my experience as I roamed alone, and I gave thanks that I was not part of an organised group.

Day 14, Friday 16th June
Warburton to Langho: 41 miles.
I was now in tune with the E-E route, which warned that 'After the easy cycling of the Cheshire Plain this leg marks a return to urban cycling and tougher

terrain. The early part is spent navigating through Warrington, Leigh, Atherton, Bolton, some challenging navigation through Blackburn and into the Forest of Bowland.' No wonder I needed help! Right on cue, my knight on a skinny bicycle arrived. Paul had cycled seventeen miles to reach me, then led me the forty miles to Langho before cycling home. In other words, for him it was a 100-mile run.

He would accept no payment for his services, only asking that I feed him en route. This certainly worked for me, because he knew all the best eating places frequented by cyclists. We stopped north of Horwick for coffee, where I topped up my battery, doing so again at Tockholes café when we had our lunch break. The café was a very busy and down to earth place, with warm-hearted folk serving solid meals washed down with big pots of tea. They certainly understood the needs of the walkers and cyclists who accounted for most of their customers. The area is popular with outdoors enthusiasts, Darwen Moor and the surrounding country lanes drawing many to this lovely part of Lancashire. It was a part of the country I had never visited, and though a dull day, weather-wise, I warmed to the area and everyone I met. Several people approached us, as we ate our lunch, and asked for my details. This was reflected in further donations to my site later on – what kind people there are!

After forty fairly challenging miles, I was delivered to the Lord Nelson Inn, where I was given a northern welcome by Darren. He led me to my warm room overlooking the Dales, and I was provided with tea and biscuits. A little gesture like a cup of tea awaiting me at the end of a long day in the saddle was always greatly appreciated. Little deeds like this, to my mind, set establishments apart.

Eating my evening meal in the inn, I wondered how Paul was getting on during his return ride home. I knew that without his help, I would probably still be trying to find my way out of Blackburn. His kindness had been a real demonstration of the camaraderie that exists between cyclists. For that, I considered, is what I had become. I was no longer a wife, mother, grandma. I had become a true cyclist! My daily routine had become second nature to me: jump onto Piro and pedal away. How many of us have such freedom? For a whole month all I had to do was to think about myself and get safely to my next destination. No thoughts about family responsibilities, shopping, cooking, cleaning and all the other happy chores that made up my normal daily life.

Day 15, Saturday 17th June
Langho to Capernwray: 43 miles
Darren pointed me in the direction of a shorter route out of Langho, with a warning of a very steep and twisting descent at the end of the lane. How

grateful I was for this advice, although I clung to my brakes as Piro and I gingerly made the descent towards Whalley.

Both books advise the same route, up to Slaidburn in the Forest of Bowland, climbing to 427 metres above sea level. I could not and still do not understand why such a route is recommended, especially as the Sustrans route then descends down to the plains before going through the valleys of the Lake District. With most heavy traffic taking the M6, I am sure there are safe roads from Warrington through to Preston and Lancaster without the punishing climb.

It being a Saturday, there were lots of cyclists on the roads, and I was seldom without company. My spirits rose with the improving weather. Before too long I was enjoying a bacon roll at a well-known café at Dunsop Bridge in the Ribble valley. Dunsop is recognised as the geographic centre of Great Britain and is very popular with cyclists, even boasting cycle sheds under which to park your bike. One of the cyclists in the café asked me if I was heading for Slaidburn and told me that I would definitely need my battery today. He was right!

I enjoyed a spectacular day of cycling through farmland and fields, enclosed with impressive stone walls, in which farmers were busy haymaking. Their equipment ranged from the ultra-modern to the traditional, machinery that is fast becoming the preserve of a bygone age. Nearly gone are the days of small conventional bales man handled onto trailers, and off again into barns. Either the labour is no longer there, or the labourers are fussier, but the bottom line is that mechanisation has overtaken farming, and nowadays one needs a degree in computers before even starting up a tractor!

The smell of freshly turned hay accompanied me as I climbed steadily upwards, watching Piro's battery drain steadily downwards. I arrived at Slaidburn, with its impressive war memorial, where I stopped to pay my respects to the lost men of the region, who had given their tomorrows for my today in this beautiful part of their country. My battery needed charging, so I headed towards a local ancient inn and ordered some lunch. I felt that, so far, I had had quite a hard day; it must have drained my concentration, because, on gathering my belongings in preparation to leave, I realised that I had not put down the switch to connect my battery to the electricity. More tea was called for!

My book cautioned that the stage from Slaidburn was one of the hardest yet most spectacular sections of the trip. As I crossed a cattlegrid I viewed the road over the moors winding upwards and onwards over the Forest of Bowland towards Cross of Greet, where I stopped to take in the vistas, which seemed to stretch to eternity. I tried to identify some of the lakeland mountains which were coming into view, while to the East I could clearly recognise Pen-y-Ghent and Ingleborough. They were the first peaks I had climbed on my first backpacking week with the local hill walking club. I can still hear myself exclaiming, 'Are we really going up there?'

As I rested, savouring the marvellous panorama around me, I was aware of how different my emotions would have been had today's stage been spent cycling into the wind with no visibility. But today the Gods were with me. I continued my ride, the route levelling out then gradually starting to descend. I felt as though I was flying! Another cyclist, Peter, caught up with me and told me that he thought that *he* was fit; he had been watching me with incredulity and was glad to discover that I was on an electric bike! Noting my signs, Peter handed over £10 and told me that he was training for L'Etape. L'Etape du Tour is an organised event which allows amateur cyclists to race over the same route as a Tour de France stage. It generally takes place in July on a Tour rest day, with around 15,000 riders coming from around the world to participate. There is also a version nearer to home named L'Etape UK, where cyclists can experience challenging climbs, road closed sections – all the trappings of the French Tour.

I left Peter to his training and continued on the single-track road, passing sheep that were enjoying their warm beds of melting tarmac. The road was popular with motorcyclists too, and I was pleased to come across a couple resting on the grassy verge, their helmets emblazoned with the Saltire, so that they resembled a medieval great helm. Their bike, too, flew the Scottish flag. I needed no reminder that I was close to the border!

We lined up our two forms of transport for a photo opportunity, and though the couple seemed very interested in me, I heard no more from them afterwards. Perhaps they were giving the polite vibes to get rid of this old dear, accosting them on the high moor where they had expected some privacy!

It was now downhill, with a warm breeze on my face. The café alongside the river in Wray looked too tempting to pass by, so I recharged Piro and enjoyed an afternoon tea in the sun. Here I got talking to a fellow End to Ender who was entirely following the Sustrans route, which he admitted was not always easy to follow. He had no set timescale and often camped en route, so he clearly didn't mind getting lost once in a while!

My destination was close to hand. I crossed the Loyn Bridge spanning the river Lune and was met by the sight of families enjoying a day out along the gently flowing river below. Children were fishing, playing in rubber dinghies and splashing about, as children do. How the topography of my day had altered! I had said farewell to the last of my route's busy conurbations, had cycled over the high moors, and ended up in a pocket of England's green and pleasant land in Capernwray.

It was an easy few miles to my destination, a first class B&B, Capernwray House. I luxuriated in a deep bath, making full use of the bath crystals provided – bliss! My exhaustion was such that I had no energy to venture into the village in search of food, but Mel, my superb hostess, had provided biscuits to accompany the tea and coffee maker in my room. After my evening routine, I shut out the sun and snuggled into my cocoon. It had felt like a very long and demanding day indeed, but all was well

Day 16, Sunday 18th June
Capernwray to Appleby: 45 miles

It was no surprise to be served a beautiful breakfast, but it was a surprise when a gentleman approached my table, curious about my Welsh flag. He hailed from Caerleon, where my husband had lived for his twenty-four years before our marriage, had taught at the local school, and had known my late in-laws. Small world indeed! A donation was given, and Mel, too, later made a generous donation, recalling how she had recently lost her husband to cancer. Everywhere I went I seemed to meet people afflicted by this truly awful disease. Listening to their experiences, be it about health, cycling, or life in general, I knew that cycling LEJoG could never have been the same had I gone with an organised group.

Refreshed, I pedalled off into the bright morning sun. Soon a sign welcomed me to Cumbria, and I felt that I really was making progress. For the time being both my books were following the same route, but before long I had a choice to make. From the village of Borwick I could follow the Sustrans route 90 across the M6 and continue into the Lake District; thence I could wiggle through the Lakes on route 6 towards Natland, thereafter picking up route 70, followed by route 68, the Pennine Cycleway, which leads towards Tebay.

Or I could leave Borwick and continue up the A6070 towards Natland, before going through Kendal, Windermere, Keswick and Carlisle. What choices! I relished the idea of taking a trip down memory lane, and cycling through some of my favourite mountains. But on the other hand, I knew how busy these roads could be.

So, as in the past, I combined the routes by simply cutting out passing through the Lakes at all. I followed the E-E route to Natland and hitched up to Sustrans route 70 thereon. It being a Sunday, the roads were very busy with families on outings, and I imagined that all the roads into the Lakes would be no exception. It seemed a very easy and suitable solution and so it proved.

The ride was pleasantly enjoyable, all the more so because of the beautiful weather. Farmers were hard at it, working on their hay crops. The tar still melted on the roads, transferring to my shoes and then to my pedals, but I much preferred that to being in the rain. There were lots of ups and downs, over hills and dales and I felt a real sense of freedom and joy as I bowled along. All these hills soon took their toll on my battery, and my grumbling tummy reminded me that I too needed topping up. A pub in the village of Tebay was my salvation. Tebay is perhaps better known for its service stations, which straddle the M6 and provide quality, local food by way of meals in the restaurants and an extensive self-service shop, with loads of first class goodies to tempt travellers to open their wallets!

I became quite excited when in the distance I recognised High Cup Nick on the Pennine Way. The Pennine Way is generally split into sixteen stages, starting at Edale in the south and finishing at Kirk Yetholm on the Scottish border. In 1965 it became Britain's first official long-distance trail. It is recognised as being a challenging route across the middle of the UK. Walkers can expect to be met with huge, deep peat hags; in dry conditions these present no problem, but when it is wet they can prove a slog, the clumpy peat clinging to your walking boots. Other stretches offer easy walking over vast stretches of moorland, where paving slabs and wooden walkways have been installed to make the experience more comfortable. The horizons stretch endlessly into the distance, the well-known peaks of the Lake District to the west, the industrial towns of yesteryear to the east.

I pondered all of this as I continued on my ride, wondering if I would get around to completing the four sections remaining for me to claim my free glass of beer at the Border Hotel, Kirk Yetholm. The late Alfred Wainwright, a famous hill walker, promised to fund this gesture for any walker who completed the trail. I wasn't sure if doing it in sections counted though. Probably not!

With the very hot weather, I was cycling in a pair of lycra cycle shorts, which my grandmother would have considered no more than a pair of black gym knickers!

Normally I wore my cut off walking shorts on top, because, with their many pockets, they had room for handkerchiefs, phone, ready cash and all the other bits and pieces it is useful to have to hand. I certainly topped up my vitamin D levels as I ground upwards towards Appleby.

Near the town I was met with a sign notifying me of the Appleby Fair, an annual gathering of gypsies and travellers which is held in the town every June. I had just missed this big event, the largest horse fair in the world, which was set up by charter in the reign of James II and has been an annual event ever since. The town was quiet, dozing under the heat. The flags which bedecked the main streets hung listlessly, but my welcome at the Royal Oak Inn was quite the opposite. Residents were sitting in the gardens, enjoying their Sunday afternoon, when this bedraggled woman came in wearing what must have looked like underwear! Nevertheless, the landlord approached me with the words, 'Coom in lass, we're expecting you, what can I get you to drink?'

Worldwide, people are welcoming towards travellers, but I mean no offence to anyone when I say that the further north I travel, the more I find people to be open and friendly. There is a warmth to their personalities which feels truly genuine, and my host was no exception.

Soon my panniers were installed in my room, which had French windows opening onto lush lawns. I thought that nothing was as marvellous and refreshing as my cool shower; well apart from the lager which followed maybe! It was bliss to get some washing done and dried, and to have time to relax and look back on a varied day. A phone call home reminded me that it was Father's Day, and my family was gathered at Helen's for dinner. Messages and donations were still arriving, and Hugh said that I had received £100 from the Monmouth Rotary Club – amazing! That evening I recorded on my blog that I was now over halfway to John o' Groats.

Day 17 Monday, 19th June
Appleby to Brisco, near Carlisle: 40 miles.

The sun continued to shine. I left Appleby for Carlisle following cycle route 71, which took me through several little valleys of undulating lanes. Before Penrith I happened upon Broughton Hall, a fourteenth-century country house associated with Broughton Castle. A sign said that dogs and cyclists were welcome, and as I ticked one of the boxes, I stooped down to access the grounds through the small arched wooden doorway. The postman was doing his rounds and took a photo of me alongside the hall's famous door knocker, of a twelfth-century design. I took a breather at the wonderful café to be found in the inner courtyard, and wandered a while through its various art and craft shops. I can recommend the homemade cakes and coffee, and it was pleasant to take a few more traditional 'touristic moments' in the pleasant surroundings.

I travelled onwards through Penrith, which I was glad to negotiate without any problems. The quiet country lanes were laden with the aromas of honeysuckle, dogroses and elderflowers. Road signs were of the old-fashioned fingerpost type, with artistic crowns atop them. I came upon a few routes that were barred because of roadworks, but Piro and I were able to pass the barriers and carry on. Birds were chirping away, as contented with the day as I was. I had now left the Pennines and Lakeland hills, which meant that the border was getting closer.

The route from Penrith to my night's lodgings led me through flat, uninteresting agricultural land, with the hum of the M6 motorway often in the background. I stumbled on my lodgings right on a crossroads, where the owners kindly offered to provide a simple supper, as there were no pubs nearby. This was one of the few occasions, upon organising my trip, when I had been unable to pre-arrange any evening food. The solution would have been to carry on towards Carlisle, but with my dread of big towns, I wanted to approach this challenge fresh, in the morning. There is no doubt that, had I had company, I would have made other decisions, but without support I had to look after myself, and in doing so, hopefully I would be prepared for whatever the next day had in store.

As usual, events turned out well. I shared a table with a Belgian cyclist who was exploring the north west of England, on a route that his English wife had worked out for him. It seemed strange that he had had no input into his route, which, to my mind, sounded rather boring. He sounded a bit fed up with his lot, which had been compounded by the severest sunburn I have ever seen. He shone like a lobster! Kindly, my hosts returned the costs of my dinner towards my charity. I noted that my husband's firm, which was sponsoring me per mile, had made my one hundredth donation. Hugh's note read: 'Keep going, lass!'

*

Day 18, Tuesday 20th June
Briscoe to Lockerbie: 36 miles

In spite of having been given directions to negotiate my way around Carlisle, of course I went wrong! How I wished that I was more competent with my phone; at times it would have made following the route so much easier. Somehow I found myself crossing the M6 and heading for Longtown; I knew that this was not right, as I wanted to be on the lower side of the motorway following Sustrans route 7. Eventually I re-routed myself and all was well. I rode parallel to the M6 as it crossed the river Esk, on what used to be the original road connecting England and Scotland, and before I knew it, Scotland itself was welcoming me. It was an emotional moment: not only was I 'home', I had reached a milestone in my journey.

I stopped at the 'Welcome to Scotland' sign, hoping that someone would pass who could take a photo of me, but the place was deserted. Naturally I could have taken a selfie, but the simple act of doing so never occurred to me! Then a couple of buses drew up and I was surrounded by a hoard of American tourists. They were full of curiosity. Perhaps they didn't see too many scantily clad ladies riding bikes in their hometowns! Cameras clicked, money was donated, they climbed back onto their buses and departed. As I gathered myself, a trio of policemen pulled alongside. They were training for JoGLE (John o' Groats to Land's

dly offered to make me a welcome coffee. This
s very well timed. I always carried water with
e, but this morning I really felt I needed a coffee
ot to get me going.

Back on the old road, it was a dull plod along
dless miles of featureless terrain, the monotony
oken only by the hum of traffic from the
otorway. At one point my route took me right
ext to the motorway and I reflected on how the
d road would look if it had to cope with today's
olume of traffic. I managed to take a photograph
at included low flying jets whizzing overhead, a
ain rumbling its way south and endless lorries
harging north and south.

My destination was a motel just off the
motorway, at Abbingdon. It was functional and
usy and also offered some shops and eateries. I
njoyed my first Harry Ramsden fish and chips and
ought a national newspaper. I didn't need to do
much work on the next day's route, so I indulged
myself, catching up on the news and a crossword.

Hugh's evening was more convivial; he rang
rom a friend's garden where a BBQ was in full
swing, and despite the miles, with all the wishes
and toasts shouted down the line, it was clear the
wine was flowing. Did I feel a bit left out, wishing
that I was one of the merry crowd of revellers? No,
I was still savouring every moment of my
adventure. The Highlands were drawing closer,
and my love of my trip was only growing. Had I

street, remarkable for its statues of a small flock of
sheep, reminding the visitor that they were in the
Southern Uplands, an area known for sheep.
Lockerbie had been home to Scotland's biggest
lamb market, and the arrival of the Caledonian
Railway only increased its importance in the sheep
industry. Before the railways, the town had been a
staging post on the Glasgow to London route, and
for me, it was my staging post for the evening.

My arrival was of some embarrassment to me.
As I was about to sweep into the reception area, I
pulled on my brakes as I noted that I was about to
trespass upon a wake. Black-clad figures abounded,
and to turn up in my usual end-of-the-day state of
disarray seemed rather disrespectful. Parking Piro
around the side of the hotel, I made my way to
reception, where the friendly staff took over and
soon had me installed in my spacious room.

It had been a sobering day. The news about Jim,
my reflections on the Lockerbie Bombing, almost
gate-crashing a funeral wake – all served to remind
me of the fragility of life around us. And bad news
had not yet finished with me. Later, as I sat in a
quiet corner of the garden with a drink and the local
newspaper, an elderly lady approached. She had
seen my arrival, and besides wanting some
company and to express her interest in my ride, she
told me that she always addressed cyclists to warn
them of the perils of not wearing a crash helmet.

Her story was that one evening, while waiting

to be called in for the family's dinner, her grandson had hopped on his bike to go for a short spin. His wheel had caught the kerb and he had fallen off his bike, badly injuring his head. As a result of the accident, he had been in hospital for ten months and his life had been shattered forever. He normally did wear a helmet, but this had just been 'a short spin before dinner'. It is a tale that I now pass on myself, knowing how easy it is to think there is a difference between leaving for a long ride and 'popping around to the shops'. Think of the similarity of not wearing a seat belt for such a trip. My tumble, in training, had reinforced to me the importance of this lady's message, so she was preaching to the converted, but I let her speak, feeling that, in her small way, she was still trying to cope with her personal disaster.

A good meal and a dram bucked me up. I made contact with my cousins in Cambuslang, with whom I would soon be having a couple of days' rest. Then I prepared my bags for the following day, which was forecast to be dull, and enjoyed a relaxing bath.

Day 19, Wednesday 21st June
Lockerbie to Abington: 38 miles

It was dull and wet, as forecast. To start with I found my way to the memorial of the Pan Am disaster. I was fortunate to meet the curator of the small museum, with whom I had a long chat. The grounds were kept in an immaculate c   kir
the four men who worked there, and I   wa
sobering moments contemplating the   me
of the event.   sh

The names of all those who had los
were inscribed on a huge grey wall of   er
land either side of the wall was pla   br
evergreen plants, and in front there w   m
circle with garden seats alongside, all   ne
contemplation. There were further i   ol
plaques and stones, and impressive head   v
off against the floral borders. The headsto   th
in Scottish cemeteries generally impart   tr
information that it is like a history le   c
reading them. Details of a wife may in
maiden name; a man's headstone will o   r
his occupation and sometimes the reaso   b
death.   e
                                             b
It was time to cast aside my sobering
four hours and to think about happiness ag   r
all, I would soon meet my clan. The old roa   r
in pre-motorway days linked Englar
Scotland, is now the Sustrans NCN route
deserted. I took a small detour towards the
of Beattock, where the road signs promise
would find refreshments, but alas this was
case. There seemed to be no tea shops and th
was closed. By now it was pouring with ra
I was sitting under the hotel porch munchi
sandwich when the owner popped out an

been following the E-E Route as a strong and younger cyclist, I may have stopped over at Moffat, which I had passed twenty miles before, and then done stage ten, Moffat to Loch Lomond, eighty-five miles away, a route the guide succinctly describes as 'hard'. But I was taking my time about things, enjoying the adventure of every day dishing up a different experience.

Day 20, Thursday 22nd June
Abington to Cambuslang: 36 miles

I was on the road by 8am, wearing three layers of my warmest clothing as I cycled into a cold northerly wind blowing across the Lowther Hills. Moorland stretched endlessly, and on a dull, cold day, Scotland was not looking its best! I wanted to be ahead of myself because I had a meeting with my aunt and uncle at the Chatelherault Country Park outside Hamilton. My aunt, who was now in her late eighties, had always been full of zest and energy. But I had not seen her or my uncle for some time and wondered how I would find them.

I need not have had concerns. We had an emotional meeting, with what the Scots would say a lot of 'greetin or bubblin' (crying). They had been as concerned about me as I had about them. Before long we were in the warm café where I thawed out, and we caught up on family news. Aunt Margaret wanted a go on my bike. I told her it would be better if she just posed on it, as it was quite heavy and very different from what she had, in her younger days, been used to.

Two years later, I sent her birthday card with a photo of her, sporting my helmet and high visibility jacket astride Piro, with the caption 'Nifty at Ninety'. I hope I have inherited some of her genes!

I was now in urban surroundings, following the road signs to Cambuslang, where I was assured a great reception at my cousin's home. I had noticed that, since I had crossed the border, Sustrans routes were more abundant and so much clearer to follow. Instead of signs giving simply the route number, I now had the luxury of the name of the next town and the mileage to reach there. This was wonderful, confirming or contradicting my assessment of my day and keeping me on track.

Hugh and I have, over the years, enjoyed the hospitality of my cousin Margaret and her husband Gus on many occasions, often motoring up in January for Burns Night suppers. These suppers are held to mark the birth of Robert Burns, who was born in Ayrshire on January 25th, 1759. He is regarded as the national bard of Scotland, and every year, from two weeks before to two weeks after his birth date, his life is celebrated in a mystical ritual known as Burns Night. These nights can be formal or low-key, but the basic format is always the same. A chairman welcomes the guests, who stand and clap as a piper leads in those who are to sit at the top table. This sets the tone for the evening. With formal gatherings the dress code suggests evening wear, with many ladies wearing full length dresses and the gentlemen looking smart in Highland regalia. Those who opt for a more relaxed style will generally wear a sprig of heather or piece of tartan pinned to their clothing.

On the first Burns Night Hugh and I attended, we were given a wonderful welcome from the chairman, but Hugh felt that, dressed in a lounge suit, he had not done justice to the event. The following morning found us in Glasgow buying a kilt of Welsh tartan, along with the rest of the Highland outfit. Thus he was equipped to attend all the Burns gatherings to follow! In 1990 I had bought a straight black dress of three-quarter length with three quarter length sleeves; it is the epitome of 'the little black dress', and worn with my tartan sash, has served me well over many Burns Nights throughout the world.

But let us return to Burns Night itself. All evenings follow the same pattern, be it a small social gathering or an event of a couple of hundred people. When the chairman has his guests settled, someone will give a recitation of 'the Selkirk Grace', which was composed by Burns. A piper then pipes in the haggis, which is held aloft by the chef, who marches around the room followed by someone carrying bottles of whisky. This is quite a ceremony in itself, but it is just the start! Next a guest enthusiastically addresses the haggis by saying this poem...

Fair fa' your honest, sonsie face
Great Chieftain o' the Puddin-race!
Aboon them a' ye tak your place,
Painch, tripe, or thairm, etc.

The haggis, which has probably been encased in animal intestine, is then stabbed with a dagger with which the speaker has been threatening it throughout his address! The contents of the haggis spill out and are served with turnips and potatoes, referred to as neeps and tatties.

The chief guest delivers a speech, 'To the Immortal Memory', a commemoration of Burns' enduring spirit. The speech can vary from the light-hearted to the literary but will always combine warmth, reflection and wit, as well as references to the Bard's life and poems. This really does sound like some weird tribal ritual, but in Scotland anything to do with Burns is taken seriously. There is a Burns federation, and his home in Ayrshire has been turned into a museum which houses over five thousand Burns artefacts. It follows that Burns has been good for the tourism industry. But what about the man himself? By the time he had died, at the age of thirty-seven, he had fathered twelve children by four different mothers, most of them illegitimately. Today's press would have a field day!

I was not prepared for what I encountered as I arrived in Cambuslang. I wheeled around the corner into the main street to find a crowd of folk waving Saltires, whooping and clapping. What was going on? What had I cycled into? I then recognised Gus and some other relatives. They had all turned out to give me the most wonderful and unexpected welcome!

'Gus, what's this all about?' I asked, as I pulled off my helmet.

'We've got used to meeting you during your escapades,' he said, 'so we couldn't simply just let you arrive at the house without a good welcome!'

He reminded me how he and Margaret had come to Stirling to bring me back to their home at the end of the Cape Wrath Trail, a two hundred mile hike up the West Coast of Scotland that I had undertaken as my sixtieth birthday present to myself. They had also collected me from Dumbarton when I had finished my ten-day circular walk known as 'the Highland Round'. For this adventure, Jennifer and I had boarded the overnight sleeper from London, alighting the following morning at Upper Tyndrum in the Highlands. We had then undertaken a ten-day backpacking expedition which encompassed the high mountains in a triangle from Upper Tyndrum to Glencoe, ending at Rannoch Station from where we took the train to Dumbarton. Gus and Margaret had so often been my back up and support, and here they were yet again, ready to do whatever they could for me.

It was a lovely feeling to have company and to enjoy a meal together. Piro was pushed into their garage, with Gus promising to check it over before I left. My bed soon beckoned and two days of rest lay ahead.

Day 21, Friday 23rd June
Rest Day at Cambuslang

Was it because I knew that I had a day off that I awoke feeling so tired? I wondered how I would have coped had I needed to continue cycling.

Margaret had booked a sport's massage at a beauty parlour in town, and didn't the masseuse know her trade! She got rid of every knot in my legs and shoulders, and after an hour on her table I emerged upright and floating on a cloud. There was nothing left for me to do but to enjoy the afternoon in my cousin's secluded garden, with an occasional glimpse of the Campsie Fells afforded me between the swaying tree branches.

In the evening the train took us into the centre of Glasgow, where I had another emotional reunion with other cousins as well as my lively aunt and uncle, who were as up for a night on the town as the rest of us. Glasgow was heaving. I felt like a country mouse, but not quite of the 'wee timorous beastie' variety. Before too long the evening was over and we were all taking trains to our respective homes, my intrepid aunt and uncle having arranged for their taxi to meet them when they got off at their station. I made a note that, if I became saddle sore in my old age, I should take up bowls. Was this the recipe for their joie de vivre?

Day 22, Saturday 24th June
Rest Day at Cambuslang

I was feeling more relaxed. Gus brought the newspapers and we had a leisurely Scottish breakfast of Ayrshire bacon, square sausages and black pudding. Why has Ayrshire bacon got the most delicious and unique taste? After all, a pig is a pig! But then again, I know for a fact our Welsh lamb tastes better than any other. Anyway, breakfast was a lot different than my normal energy-fuelled fare, and I made the most of it.

I was asked if I wanted to go through to Edinburgh to see the Royal Highland Agricultural Show, or perhaps take a car run down the Clyde. I know how exhausting walking around a big show can be, and I had to remind myself to make the most of this rest. Later we walked down to the River Clyde for Gus to point out the start of my route the next day. Both my guidebooks were following the same Sustrans route, 75, but the maps in the E-E book were exceptional, even to the extent that I could pick out my cousin's street.

In the evening we watched television. Margaret had recorded a programme about Billy Connolly, remarking that 'Mum can't stand him'. I did not tell her that he was not my favourite entertainer either!

However, I did know that his likeness had recently been painted on the sides of Glasgow tenements, by three different well-known artists, including Jack Vettriano. Margaret was aware that I admired Vettriano's work, to the extent that I had just finished my own version of his *Singing Butler*, which I had painted for my daughter's birthday.

I shared a connection with the famous artist, in that he was born in Methil, a small suburb outside the town of Leven, in Fifeshire. I had spent a lot of time there during the first five years of my life, when I had been looked after by my maternal grandparents during my mother's illness. My grandmother had lost a leg in an industrial accident, so she clumped around with a wooden replacement. I slept in the same bed as her and thought there was nothing irregular in her taking off her leg every night and propping it up on the wall next to the bed.

My grandfather was unusual too. He slept in a big walk-in cupboard which in Scotland is called a 'press'. He had been a miner all of his life, and it was as a miner that he had served in World War One. He had been gassed, and it was said that on his return from the war he was never the same again. In addition, he had lost several fingers on both hands. It was his life in the trenches that resulted in his sleeping in what he called his 'dug oot'. There was just enough space for a bed to be wedged in between the walls, with shelves going around, on which he kept a tin mug and other bits and pieces. In spite of his physical handicap, he could still perform magic tricks with his mangled hands and was renowned for telling stories. The children in the neighbourhood used to come to the door to ask, 'Is Papa Wright coming out to play?'

Both my grandparents were greatly affected by having lost two daughters within a year, both to TB. It was then that my grandfather had started to drink heavily, and as a child I have memories of him lying paralytic in the hallway, having been carried home from the pub. On such evenings, I would be bundled off to spend the night at the neighbours up the stairs. I suppose that in today's society, social services would have had a lot to say about my upbringing. For me, it was simply part of the fabric of my life.

After two days of good food, fellowship and some culture thrown in, I felt refreshed and ready for the road again.

Day 23, Sunday 25th June
Cambuslang to Balloch: 30 miles

It is sound advice to start out on a Sunday. The roads tend to be quieter, and there is time to adjust to the route and settle in for the start of another stage. Gus had cleaned and oiled Piro, and I too was clean and rested and firing on all cylinders. We rolled down the roads toward Sustrans route 75, which ran along the Clyde. This would later become route 7, which would keep me company for many miles ahead.

My morning's travel only reinforced my admiration for Scotland's route signs, which indicated the miles to the next place of interest, and how long it would take by bike or walking. I always knew that I was on track, and when I came to the many bridges which crossed the Clyde, I had time to stop and appreciate the architecture, and to read the information provided on the plaques often found alongside. With my bike parked up, my flags fluttering, walkers with dogs and families pushing prams often stopped to exchange a few words and donate to my cause.

I later passed the *Waverly* steamer, docked on the opposite bank, and stopped to have a good look at her. For my aunt Margaret's sixtieth wedding anniversary, my cousin had asked me if I could paint a canvas of the Waverly leaving Millport. There is a painting of this in the house the family have rented every Easter for time immemorial, and 'wee Margaret' thought that it would be wonderful if a replica could be hung in her mum and dad's house – no pressure then! I studied my subject in detail, and in the end would receive my reward when my uncle Mark peered at the gift and remarked, 'I can see you got the funnels at the right angle!'

Although my two guidebooks covered the same cycle route, the difference in the information within them was vast. Certainly you won't get lost following the Sustrans guide, but it bore no comparison to the Cicerone 'End to End' guide. In it, I read about the history of Glasgow and the reasons why, through its shipbuilding industry, it had become famous throughout the world. The information was enough to keep me engrossed within the pages, but not too much to be overpowering. It certainly enriched my experience as I cycled along this route steeped in history, the development of which my family had, in some small way, played an important part in.

I knew Papa Campbell, my paternal grandfather, as an ancient, grey-haired man, yet he was only sixty-six when he died in 1951. Born in 1885, he had started work in 1911 for what was then known as the Board of Trade, later to become the Ministry of Labour. By 1916 he was head of the Clydebank branch, a position he held for the rest of his working life. Throughout his employment, he would have seen Clydeside and the shipbuilding industry go through many ups and downs. In 1913 the River Clyde boasted thirty-nine shipyards and launched almost a fifth of the world's shipping tonnage. The ship *the Queen Mary* had been started in the famous John Brown's Shipyard in 1930, but by the end of the following year work on her had stopped due to the Great Depression. By 1934 a loan had been obtained which enabled work to continue, so it was all hands on deck to get ahead with finishing her. Besides being responsible for placing many thousands of men in employment, Papa Campbell's biggest claim to fame came in 1934, when, within just two days, he recalled 3,000 workers to enable the continuation of the building the *Queen Mary*. In pre-computer days this was no mean feat. When the ship was ready to be launched, the River Clyde had to be deepened to cope with her size. For services rendered, my grandfather was awarded the King George Jubilee Medal. Some grumpy old man!

Amongst other firms for which he was responsible for recruiting labour was the Royal Ordnance Factory at Dalmuir, on Clydeside. One such employee was his son, my father, Archie. But Archie was not a conscientious student and failed to keep up his attendance at night school. Consequently he was fired! He was told to call to collect his cards, but fate intervened and taught him a lesson he would never forget. In March 1941, Clydebank was devastated by the first of several air attacks by the Luftwaffe, with the ROF one of its targets. Besides damage to the factory, all the wages and personnel records were also destroyed. This let Archie off the hook, and he returned to his work a more diligent person!

I mulled over my family history as the Scottish Exhibition and Conference Centre, known as the Clyde Auditorium Centre, came into view. I could see the magnificent crane, the last one left on

Clydeside, towering over the modern buildings that have come to dominate the redevelopment of the area. It stood, a lone sentinel, a testament to bygone days. It was approaching coffee time and I swept into the crowds who were milling about outside. I parked alongside a coffee stall. Immediately, drawn by my flags, several families approached me, the children wanting to look at my dragon. The parents soon grasped what I was doing, and money was proffered without hesitation. How did the Scots get a reputation for being mean?

While I was enjoying my bacon butty, a senior gentleman approached me, again drawn by my dragon. 'I see your flag,' he said, 'don't suppose you know Newport?' I said that it was a town some fifteen miles from my home and that yes, I used to know it very well. Not only had I used to work there, but my brother had been a fitter on the buses of Newport Corporation Transport Department. I thought my new acquaintance was about to hug me! 'Come with me, let me show you my bus,' he said.

Of all the invitations that I received en route, this was a first! I had stumbled upon an exhibition of vehicles staged by Glasgow Vintage Vehicle Trust. My new friend, Scott Crichton, led me towards one of the old vintage red buses and explained it had been on loan to Newport Transport Department as a driver/trainer bus from 1992 to

2002, and my informant had driven the bus from Newport to the Glasgow museum at the end of the loan. There was a certificate adhered to the door which verified this information. Newport must have left an impression on the chap, because his excitement in speaking to me was genuine. We chatted for a little while, and at the end of our conversation, without hesitation he presented a £20 note. His mate repeated the gesture, and together they waved me on my way to my lunch stop at the Dug Café, a dog-friendly cafe at Bowling Basin.

I still cycled along memory lane, passing signs for Partick, Clydebank, Loch Lomond, names I associated with my Glasgow childhood.

I had lived with my paternal grandparents in Knightswood, where I attended the local school, situated on the Boulevard of Great Western Road. We lived nearby, on the edge of a huge park, and my journey to school consisted of Gran walking me across the road in front of the house, putting a stick in my hand, and sending me on my way! The stick was to rattle across the metal railing which ran all the way around the park; as long as I kept this up, after almost a mile I should arrive at the lollipop lady, who would see me across the busy road and tram lines. I repeated this walk every day without thinking there was anything unusual about it. When it was foggy, as it often was, it was only the sound of the clang-clang of my stick which guided me to my destination. Nowadays this would be regarded as neglectful. But there was no jumping out of a 4x4 after a mile ride to school for me!

I encountered a sign telling me that that it was 215 miles to Inverness and nineteen miles to Loch Lomond. Mention of Inverness made me smile and hug myself. I really was going to do this! The canal path along the Forth and Clyde canal was now my highway. Opened in 1790, it travels thirty-eight miles from Grangemouth, in the east of Scotland, to Bowling, in the west, where it joins the Clyde. In its day it was a vital link through the industrial belt of Glasgow, but like many canals it has fallen into disrepair.

Soon I spied the Erskine Bridge ahead and knew that lunch was not far away. Prior to the opening of the bridge in 1971, the only way to cross the Clyde was by ferry. I cycled under the bridge and headed for Bowling Harbour. It proved to be a delightful spot, the result of the area having been restored to life through millions of pounds of investment. Under railway arches small shops have sprung up, amongst which was a bicycle shop, and the famous Dug Café.

During my intrepid childhood, when my mother was in hospital and father working, I spent time with Uncle Bob and Aunt Mae and my cousin Robert, in Reading, England. Uncle Bob was a fairly well-known Scottish footballer, having started his career with Falkirk in 1941. He played for them for six years before moving to Chelsea, for whom he made 188 appearances between 1947 and 1954. In today's world he would probably have been very famous – and rich! His proudest moments in his career were winning five caps for the Scotland National team between 1947 and 1950.

My time in Reading left me with a fear of dogs, which I have been unable to overcome. I can still feel a panic when I recall, as a four-year-old, a bulldog jumping up at me. With my small stature its nose and eyes were level with mine, and I thought I was about to be eaten alive! Ever since, when I am in the company of strange dogs, I simply freeze, and no doubt the dogs can sense this. And I was now about to have lunch in the Dug Café. For those of you not up to speed with your Scots, 'dug' translates to 'dog'. A whole café dedicated to dogs!

Trish, a good friend of my daughter, Jennifer, had arranged to meet me, and she arrived with her Shih Tzu into what appeared to be a dog's paradise. Dog bowls, dog biscuits, dog everything! But the food for humans was very good too. It was lovely to see Trish again. She lavished gifts upon me – soap, tissues, energy tablets and face wipes: anything she thought I would find useful – then added in a healthy donation. I even stroked her dog!

I was glad that I had no need to frequent Magic Cycles, a smart-looking bicycle shop just along from the café. Route 7 led me onwards towards

Balloch, with my E-E guide giving clear instructions, especially where caution was needed getting through Dumbarton. What a splendid spot this was! It was an enjoyable ride following the river Leven northwards. The Highlands were now so close, and my excitement mounted with every pedal.

My destination was a Marsden Hotel, where Piro spent the evening in the laundry room. I set about my evening routine then donned what glad rags I had with me, hailed a taxi and headed for Renton, a village I had cycled past earlier in the afternoon. I had a dinner date with our friends Lena and Tom.

It was an evening I will never forget, for many reasons. Hugh and I had met this couple on a cruise in Asia several years before. They were on our table in the evening, and we quickly took to each other. Our friendship was cemented during an extended stay in the same hotel in Hong Kong.

Tom suffered from macular degeneration and his sight was limited, but he certainly did not let this stop his enjoyment of life. He was a true gentleman and a wonderful raconteur. Hugh and I so enjoyed this couple's good company. Our friendship amounted to visits when we were in Scotland, and cards and letters at Christmas, yet there was always a comfortable bond between both our families.

That evening, I received the warmest of

welcomes to their home, where I enjoyed a memorable candle-lit dinner. I recorded that they both looked well, but that Tom, aged ninety-three, was suffering from cancer. Remarkably, though, both he and Lena still had the same cheerful disposition. We nattered about so many things, and I was especially interested in their grandson, who had recently cycled LEJoG with friends. Having followed his trip, they were overawed about me doing it solo.

As I left, I was handed a generous donation. I climbed into the taxi and waved good-bye, and sadly it would be the last time that I would see Tom. He died not long afterwards.

It was a balmy evening, the sky still bright at 11.00pm. I felt that Scotland had been keeping such perfect conditions especially for me. How easily I was fooled!

Day 24 Monday, 26th June
Balloch to Killin: 58 miles

Both my guidebooks told me that the next stage offered the most magnificent scenery of the entire journey. My E-E route left Balloch on the busy A82 leading to Glencoe, with the warning that tourist coaches (lots of them), as well as HGV lorries, cars and motorbikes filled the roads in summer. Reading this again I remembered why I had chosen to continue on Sustrans route 7, which would instead take me through Balloch Castle Country

Park, the Queen Elizabeth Forest Park and the Trossachs National Park.

On paper, this run had sounded idyllic, but I should have thought a bit more about the terrain, and asked myself about the practicalities of undertaking such a stretch on my own. I would be more vulnerable than I had ever been, and any problems encountered on an isolated stretch would have been bad news indeed. There was a weather warning forecast for the following few days, and it was time to re-assess the situation and up my pedal power. I decided to cancel my booking at Callander, where I had planned to arrive after a comfortable thirty-four miles and to push on to Killin. There I made a reservation at the Courie Inn for two nights, which also meant abandoning the following evening's stay. In both cases, when I rang to cancel my bookings, both my hosts graciously said that they would not charge me. I had not mentioned that I was cycling for charity, nor my age or anything which would influence them towards treating me with some compassion. No, I was simply a lady cyclist on my own, who thought it prudent to alter my itinerary in view of the forecasted storm. With their kind words of care, I set off on my ambitious plan to cycle sixty miles!

The weather throughout the day was fine, affording long distance views. To start with, pedaling through Balloch Castle Country Park was all that had been promised, smooth paths eventually opening on to country roads. Thereafter undulating lanes led me along my route, also known as the Lochs and Glens North. I had planned a coffee stop at Aberfoyle, known as the Gateway to the Highlands. Impressive, high mountains came into view as I flew down some very steep country lanes, giving thanks for the clear visibility that allowed me to appreciate the spectacular scenery.

Aberfoyle has become a tourist hot spot, with a Scottish Wool Centre, a big visitor's centre, and the usual cafés and hotels, but I had been advised not to follow in the tourists' footsteps and to stop at a small, old fashioned tearoom on the main street. This was good advice. I topped up on delicious homemade cake and coffee, in readiness for my adventure through the Queen Elizabeth Forest Park.

Leaving the café I carried on up the hill on the A827 before turning right, into the forest. There I was met with several signs drawing visitors' attention to what the park had to offer: there was a route for cars, and several for mountain and road bikes to choose between. A notice asked the reader, 'Are you suitably prepared?' Of course, I was!

I was approached by a cyclist who pointed out that my bike stand was down. I was so grateful to be told this, as it could very easily have caught on the road and unseated me. I wondered how I had managed to cycle from the teashop with no mishap. 'Take your time, girl,' I admonished myself. Clearly my mind was on the long day ahead.

My guidebook told me that the terrain, as far as Callander, was a mixture of gravel and stony paths, and when the path followed Loch Venacher it became rough and stony. It didn't say how stony was stony!

My alternative would have been to continue on the main road leading to the Trossachs and Loch Katrine and along the north side of Loch Vanacher, but I knew that this would be a busy route, and less fun. Careful what you wish for!

I set off through the forest on well-maintained, wide, undulating tracks. The words 'rough and stony' niggled in my mind, but I reasoned that, as this was a route recommended by my Sustrans book, there was nothing to be overly concerned about.

Passing Loch Drunkie I stopped for a breather and listened to the silence. Giant pine trees surrounded the loch, and with the still atmosphere, I felt alone in the world. I thought this was much better than holding my breath as lorries passed me on the A road.

That is, until I reached the forewarned stony section! Oh yes, my path was also described as 'smaller' than average; I would go as far as saying that it was pretty well non-existent. I could not believe that I was on the designated track; the stones were so chunky that I feared that my 80% puncture proof tyres might say 'enough'. But no, it was the correct route because, as promised, it led to a private road which in turn took me to Callander. There I stopped for lunch, not because I was hungry, but because I felt that I ought to top up Piro's battery, and I wanted to re-read what section two of my day had to offer.

I paid attention to outlines of the afternoon section, especially where my map indicated an exclamation mark with 'steep stony path' written noted alongside. Otherwise the route seemed appealing, because it left the town on the old Callander to Oban railway line, promising a pleasant ride along the loch shore with views over to Ben Ledi. That sounded good, and the picture of the Glen Ogle Viaduct looked especially attractive. 'When in doubt do nought' has always been my mantra, so even after all these considerations, I resolved to keep to the main road.

After a quick bite and with a recharged battery, I set off on the road. I had not gone far before, on a twisty bend, a tourist bus passed much too close for comfort. Near the Falls of Lenny I changed my mind and crossed over to another route. I immediately congratulated myself on my good decision, as I had the track on the old railway line to myself. 'If it's like this all the way, this is wonderful,' I enthused. It was not to be. The track eventually gave way to a path which zigzagged up the hillside. In my notes I recorded that 'I pushed Piro up a bracken-strewn hill side which was reminiscent of my hill walking days.' By the time I reached the top I was exhausted. Granted, the views over Loch Earn were spectacular; the cars below on the A85, where I would have been had I followed the main road, looked like small toys.

When I reached the level section and mounted Piro, I was just starting to pedal when I noticed two figures emerging from the forest, wearing black face masks! They looked to have guns slung over their shoulders. Terror struck me. I remembered having read about the discovery of an Al Qaeda training camp in the Lake District, and for a moment wondered if I had tumbled upon one in the remote Highlands. Was this the end of me? I decided to boldly cycle forth and ignore these two strangers, who were walking towards me. As they neared, I realised that the masks were nothing more sinister than midge nets worn to protect from the dreaded insects that plague the country between May and September. Nevertheless, meeting two strangers in a remote area had unnerved me, and for the first time during my whole ride I started to glance over my shoulder and to question the sanity of doing this on my own.

I was now on a gentle downhill section, cycling over the viaduct. I was, as ever, conscious about conserving my battery, so I freewheeled as much as possible, before crossing the main road into a forestry plantation leading me towards Killin. I had now become so paranoid about rough stony tracks and masked men that I never wanted to cycle in a forest again! I pushed Piro through most of the track, fearing a puncture at the end of a very long and stressful day. My relief was enormous when I found myself on a normal road!

I passed the impressive Falls of Dochart, which flow through the town, and headed for my two-night stop at the Courie Inn. *Coorie* is a Scottish word meaning to snuggle up, and I was more than ready to do this expression justice. I felt as though my legs would hardly hold me, as I entered this gem of an inn. The landlord immediately took charge of both me and my bike. Piro was housed in a shed, with a promise to have it cleaned up and checked before I left, and I was shown upstairs to my blissfully warm and comfortable room. Was I ready for a day off! I soaked in a warm bubble bath with a cup of tea alongside me, as my mind played over my day in the saddle. It was full of what ifs, some of them too scary to contemplate. I regretted that I had not had time en route to digress to Rob Roy's grave at Balquhidder, which I had intended to visit, and my diary recorded that I was even too tired to wash my hair or do pilates. I really needed a bit of tender loving care and thought that this might even extend to *two* glasses of wine that evening!

I had not expected to find an inn with a continental bistro atmosphere buried in the highlands. The food was delicious, and the warm and happy atmosphere was enhanced by the music that filled the dining room. It was my type of music, from smooth classics, romantic moments and sounds of the sixties. I felt lonely. Why wasn't Hugh sitting opposite and pouring the wine as we enjoyed the evening together? Why had I undertaken this mad adventure, and on my own? Until this point, I had generally been in a buoyant mood, full of zest for my adventure, but that evening I felt quite morose and lonely.

I asked the waitress about the music and was introduced to Spotify, which she downloaded to my iPad. I was soon feeling more cheerful, my mind on further adventures – although, I decided, a condition would be to share them with Hugh. I was sure that he could be persuaded to take time off from his office work and sheep and accompany me. So it was to prove. The following year we would cycle together from Roscoff in France to Santander in Spain, in brilliant weather, when my experience of having cycled LEJoG was to prove of great benefit.

But that was in the future. For now, feeling warm and replete after a relaxing evening, I cooried into my cosy room. There was poor internet reception, so I had no need to do my evening report. My mobile popped up with a loving text from my daughter, Jennifer. A perfect end to a testing day!

*

Day 25, Wednesday 27th June
Rest Day at Killin

I awoke to the rain lashing against the window. It was eight am and in normal circumstances I would have been ready to set off. But today was a rest day and I had no demands upon me but to do just that, rest. After a full Scottish breakfast I went back to bed and slept for two hours, a sure sign that I was flagging. By lunch time, in spite of the rain, I donned my wet weather gear and ventured out to have a look at the rapids and the falls which thundered through the village. After the overnight rain they looked quite spectacular. But as I found some good Wi-Fi signal and caught up on messages, my mind was clicking into overdrive: for the following couple of days, yet more gales and heavy rain were forecast.

Day 26, Wednesday 28th June
Killin to Pitlochry, 40 miles

After a super porridge and 'proper coffee' breakfast, the owner of the inn presented me with my very smart-looking bike. Everyone had been so warm-hearted and helpful, and I left a £20 tip.

Not far out of Killin I turned onto a country lane which would lead me to Kenmore. Nobody could miss the big road sign informing that the road was 'Walking and cycle friendly only'. I felt joyful at the prospect of a traffic-free, properly surfaced road. This was more like it. And no mention of forests! What bliss it was to pedal leisurely onwards, with Loch Tay on my left, and Ben Lawers and other impressive mountains towering in the background. It was a pity that the mist robbed me of seeing them in their grandeur, but at least it was dry.

Kenmore lay at the end of the loch. It boasts Scotland's oldest hotel, the Kenmore Hotel, which was opened in 1572. If walls could speak, I wondered what tales they would tell. Centuries before the Jacobite uprisings and General Wade's military roads opened up the Highlands, this area of Scotland was surely extremely isolated. Loch Tay must have been an important region in early civilisation, because twenty submerged Iron Age artificial islands have been discovered in its waters. These islands, known as crannogs, were pre-historic homes and farmsteads, made out of natural materials and reached by man-made causeways linking them to the mainland. They were also used as strongholds in time of danger. I headed for a reconstructed one at the Crannog Centre, just outside Kenmore.

I was just in time to join a group having a tour of a crannog. The guides, dressed as they would have been in bygone days, engaged the audience, including young children, who thoroughly enjoyed the roleplaying. Passing the inevitable tourist shop at the exit, I was handed contributions from some of the visitors, before going on my way.

The road out of Kenmore was quiet and level and felt like a gift. I had no concerns to worry about; I only had to pedal onwards. When I arrived, Pitlochry was humming with international holidaymakers. As I emerged from a shop, a couple from Australia, who had spotted my bike, engaged me in conversation, telling me about their trip to Scotland and their family tree research. They were so impressed with my adventure that they donated generously and said that they would follow me via my blogs.

Piro soon took me to the baronial-styled Pine Trees Hotel, just off the main street. I recorded in my diary, 'At £80 for D.B.B. this is excellent value. It is the most comfortable bed and room so far and everyone is chatty and genuinely friendly. At 11pm it is still light outside. Hugh has sold 40 kg lambs but is not too happy with the price!' Farmers never are!

Tomorrow, according to my book, I would officially enter the section named 'the Scottish Highlands', where it was warned I should be 'prepared for long and lonely stretches'. A severe storm warning had been issued. I had planned to reach Newtonmore, forty miles away, and under normal circumstances this would have presented no difficulty...

Day 27 Thursday 29th June
Pitlochry to Newtonmore: 40 miles.
The weather chart on the television news was not a happy one to behold. Scotland was covered in

dark blue. Rain and gales were forecast to last all day, with winds coming from the north. I reasoned that I had no alternative but to kit myself out for a wet day, and by 9am I was off.

There is a Scottish word called 'stoating', often used to describe heavy rain – as in, 'It's stoating down'. For the sense of the expression, imagine that when a rain drop falls on the road it makes its own little puddle, and in that puddle there is another little whirlwind puddle bouncing on top, then magnify this over a big stretch of roadway. In this situation the road ahead of me resembled a torrent of angry water jumping all over the place, and it was into this melee of angry water that I was obliged to cycle.

I was familiar with the area, having stayed nearby in my mountain walking days. The views from Ben Vrackie, which rises 2,759 feet behind the town, are some of the best from any mountain, but alas not today. To start with I was sheltered from the worst of the elements, as I headed towards the Pass of Killicrankie, just outside Pitlochry, and onwards through the Blair Atholl Estate, the bad weather no more than a nuisance to me. The estate is perhaps best known for having embraced tourism, and it is generally a very busy place, but at this early hour I glided past a wet and desolate landmark.

I left the relative comfort of low-lying land and started my gradual climb along the original military road rising through bleak moors, heading towards the Pass of Drumochter at 1,508 feet. I was sandwiched between the busy A9 road above me and the river Gary and the railway line below, and there was now no protection whatsoever. I was becoming very tired and cold, ice cold rain finding its way into every nook and cranny of my gear. My feet, in spite of my waterproof overshoes, were soaking. My hands were numb. Gloves were of no use. Piro, too, was losing energy at an alarming rate, and I fretted about having enough power to get me to the whisky distillery at Dalwhinnie, where there was food, shelter and electricity.

I was now exposed to the full force of the north wind as it tore into me, making every turn of my pedals a supreme effort. The rain pelted me with a hail of ice-cold pellets, and I wondered what to do. What could I do? I was freezing cold, wet and dispirited. I needed a hot drink to try to restore some energy in me. Ahead I spied, through my dim eyesight, (I had removed my glasses as they did not have rain wipers on them!) what I thought was a bush, and I decided that I would hunker into it for some respite. Alas, it turned out to be a reel of sheep netting propped alongside the track!

By noon I was confronting such a headstrong wind that I was pedalling to stand still. I was afraid that I would be blown off my bike, so dismounted and started to push. This was easier said than done, the wind enveloping me in a power which felt supernatural, like being in a dryer that wanted to spin me round and round. I screamed at the wind to stop, to relent for just a few moments to enable me to catch my breath, but no, it continued to enjoy tormenting me with its fury, roaring across the barren glen, like an express train, buffeting into me as I staggered along like a drunkard, clinging to Piro for support. My cape whirled up and danced around me, whacking into my face with a cold, wet shock. I began to cry. I now knew how Captain Oates had felt during Scott's ill-fated Terra Nova Expedition in 1912. When things were looking really hopeless, he left his tent and walked into the snowy wilderness. Part of me wanted to do... what? I felt so wretched that I had no resolve left.

I had never witnessed hypothermia, but I recognised the symptoms. I needed help. It was clear that I could not continue in my perilous state. Luck was with me; my route passed just below a lay-by of the A9. There was a tall container parked on its own and I made a beeline to shelter in its lea. I could feel the container swaying in the gale, the wind howling underneath its carriageway, threatening to blow both me and my bike back down the road. My hands were too cold to open my pannier to get to my flask. My phone was there too, in a waterproof case, but that too was outside my reach. I had even considered ringing 999. After deliberating, I knew that I had little alternative but to carry on, and when my battery gave out, I would re-assess my position.

I was now cycling on the track which ran alongside the busy road, the main artery to the north of Scotland. I hadn't got far when I noticed a white pickup truck in the opposite carriageway lay-by. I left Piro and risked crossing the four lanes to seek help. Readers may be thinking, 'What an irresponsible thing to do, crossing to accost a stranger for help.' The bottom line was that I needed help, and perhaps naively, being a Scot back in my homeland, I felt safe with 'my ain folk'.

Cometh the hour, cometh the man. I tapped the steamed-up window of the truck. A startled driver raised his head as he awakened from his nap. He probably thought that he was having some sort of nightmare, as he wound down the window with the words, 'Whatever's the matter, lassie?' What he thought of this drowned old woman I do not know, but he was my knight in a workman's white truck. That was more than enough for me!

I explained my predicament then asked if he could take me and my bike the three extra miles to the distillery so that I could top up Piro's battery. He replied that, in view of the appalling conditions, he would take me to my destination in Newtonmore (a further 12 miles away). Within no time we had hauled Piro and my bags into the back of the open truck and I gratefully sank into the passenger's seat beside my rescuer. We got to know each other. He was a Mr Grey, driving a white truck; I was Mrs Green riding a red bicycle, and I added that my daughter was a Mrs Brown! He told me about his family and grandchildren, adding that he drove along this route every week, delivering parts from Glasgow to Inverness, and that he had never before noticed the cycle track.

We passed the Dalwhinnie distillery and I promised to myself that, when returning home, I would cycle this gap between Newtonmore and where I had been rescued in order to fulfil my aim of truly having cycled the whole of the UK. Mr Grey refused any money for his petrol, or pocket money for his grandchildren. I don't know if he ever followed my progress, but I am indebted to him for having recued me from such a worrying situation.

My host at the Glen Hotel in the main street of Newtonmore immediately took all my soaking outer clothes and shoes and handed me a brandy. Things were looking up! Imbibing spirits at 2pm on a bleak and freezing day seemed the sensible thing to do. My room was made ready, but oh, how I longed for a bath in which to warm my freezing bones. Alas, it would be showers from now on. I justified the expression 'soaked to the skin' as the rest of my clothes slithered off, but a brisk shower and warm food restored life to my body.

Hugh broke our rule of phoning only in the mornings and evenings, having grown concerned about me when he'd seen the forecast. I was not fair to him, crying down the line, but he told me not to worry and that, in the absence of his shoulder, that's what he was there for. He reminded me that before long I would be able to have a good rest and he encouraged me onwards. My best tonic!

The gales had made the news. I later learned that the organised LEJoG ride going via Glencoe had been abandoned in view of the weather conditions. This was, as I have said, the advantage of having support and company en route. But hey, I had conquered and coped, and my timetable was still on track.

The evening was spent in the cosy bar, savouring the warmth, food and wine. There were several welcoming messages of support for me to read, plus calls from the girls. I allowed myself some small recognition of my achievement, while at the same time reflecting on my amazing good fortune to have had, yet again, people to turn to in my hour of need. Alas, I had no photographs to record this day of days, but I knew that my memories would take a long time to fade.

Day 28, Friday 30th June
Newtonmore to Carrbridge: 35 miles
The landlord presented me with my dry clothes, and I prepared to set off on a dull but cold day. I noticed that one of the plastic symbols which I had stuck to the side of one of my panniers had been ripped off during yesterday's trials. While leaving,

my eye caught a notice on the wall about some of the regulations under the Licensing (Scotland) Act 2005, which advised that smokers must leave their drinks inside while smoking outside after 9.00pm. I wondered why it was permitted to take your beer and cigarette out before 9.00pm, if the weather the day before was anything to go by!

But today the wind had abated, and the light constant drizzle was unnoticeable compared with yesterday's downpour. In Kingussie I left the main road, turning right to follow my route through Strathspey and into the Caledonian pinewoods of the Inchriach Forest. Almost immediately the ruins of Ruthven Barracks loomed ahead. I stopped to read the information on the boards outside the grounds, which informed me that they had been built in 1719 to reinforce the king's peace after the 1715 Jacobite rising – in other words to let the Scots know who was boss!

The uprising in 1715 had the aim of restoring James Stuart, the Old Pretender, to the thrones of England, Ireland and Scotland, and deposing George I, a Hanoverian monarch. The Scots, having lost, would have to wait until 1745 to have another go at upstaging what they felt to be English subjugation. Under the leadership of James' son, known as Bonnie Prince Charlie, it all came to a bad end with the defeat of the Scots at the battle of Culloden in 1746. On the retreat from Culloden, the Ruthven Barracks were destroyed.

I wanted these forlorn walls to speak to me! Having been born in 1946, I considered two hundred years prior to my birth to be within touching distance. In researching my family tree, I have managed to trace my Campbell of Argyll lineage back to 1760, to the village of Dalavich on the shore of Loch Awe. However, I also knew that my clan was not popular in Scotland; it had a knack of knowing on which side its bread was buttered, choosing whatever faction suited it best! At the battle of Culloden, four companies of the Argyll Militia, amongst other companies, fought on the government side. Oh dear!

I had once stayed at the Clachaig Inn in Glencoe, where I was met by a message, engraved in brass on the reception desk: 'No Hawkers or Campbells'. I signed under my married name, but wondered what would have happened had I signed in under my maiden one? The massacre, in 1692, of thirty members of the Clan MacDonald, still leaves a bitter taste in the mouths of Glencoe. The MacDonald Clan had offered hospitality to the visitors, the government troops led by Archibald Campbell, the 10th Earl of Argyll. During the night the government troops massacred many of their hosts, with others fleeing to perish in the freezing snow of that February night. My bloodline was not reflecting well upon me.

Under a blue sky the strath (wide valley or glen) would have looked beautiful; however I had to be content to cycle through big puddles and assess the flocks of sheep grazing under a dreary sky. Road surfaces were uniformly wet, with debris all over the place, a testament to the storm.

The scenery changed as I approached Aviemore, a one-time village which has grown into a town that attracts tourists throughout the year. It is the skiing capital of Scotland, and during snow-free months of the year it is popular with many other outdoor sports enthusiasts too. I had a feeling of lassitude about me, and welcomed a comfortable halt at the Hilton Hotel. Forgoing my morning coffee, I laid down some energy-giving carbohydrates by way of porridge, maple syrup, nuts and fresh fruit – super!

Then, to my alarm, I discovered that my iPad was not working. I wondered if the dampness of yesterday had taken its toll. The Tourist Office directed me to a shed up a side street where a helpful person said he would look at it for me, asking me to return in two hours. Many people would welcome the chance to have a couple of hours to browse around the shops, especially the abundant outdoor ones where you could easily bankrupt yourself, but my choice was to head for the library.

There I spotted Linda Bellingham's book *There's Something I've Been Dying to Tell You*, with her beautiful smiling face adorning the front page. It had received rave reviews, and here was my chance for a quick flick through the pages. I left the library feeling quite depressed, yet again giving thanks for my health, which I never take for granted. *This bloody cancer seems to get around everyone*, I thought, as I trudged back to see how my iPad was faring. Apparently, the problem had simply been that it had not been updated, and all had been rectified. Perhaps my iPad, Piro and I were all needing a bit of an overhaul. I carried on, thinking about Linda.

My choice of accommodation, Fairwinds in Carrbridge, was an unusual one for me, because it actively welcomed dogs! Hugh is allergic to cats and dogs when they are indoors, along with feathers and flowers, so when booking somewhere to stay we have to search for places which don't welcome pets. It gets more and more difficult every year, and I feel there is a market for a website offering accommodation 'Dogs not welcome'.

But the reviews for this small hotel were so good, and the stage distance for the day so perfect, I decided to book anyway. I received the warmest welcome from Janette and Peter, who immediately took care of Piro's overnight accommodation then settled me in with complementary tea and cake. A 5-star hotel could not have impressed me any more than this. It was another chance to overcome my fear of dogs and to give out an odd pat. Perhaps I would become a dog lover after all?

Once again my room was comfortable and well equipped. I could not imagine pitching a tent and getting my own meals after such a long day – perhaps if I had been forty years younger. I had already established that I could eat in a local restaurant in the village, but with its population of seven hundred, I was not expecting this small village to host a restaurant capable of producing such a meal as the Carrbridge Kitchen did. This restaurant is an undiscovered gem which would, in any bigger conurbation, be the talk of the town. Well done to the young chef who provided one of the best meals I enjoyed on my whole trip.

The evening light lingered as it does in the north of Britain, and I too lingered as I strolled along the silent road towards my digs. The village is renowned for its historic ancient stone packhorse bridge, which was built in 1717 to allow funeral processions to get to the local church, hence it being known locally as the 'coffin bridge'. There were good views of it from the main road. I imagine that in the daytime tourist buses would drop off their load of camera-clicking holiday makers for a quick snap, before driving off to the next tourist attraction. I had my own time to marvel at the weathered structure, and to think about an era when a bridge over a rushing river was the wonder of the century to the local people.

On returning to my room, I re-entered the twenty-first century by turning on my television. I watched a programme about the life of the Welsh singer Tom Jones. 'The Green, Green Grass of

Home' seemed a very long way away to me, as it did to Tom as he blasted out his lament. I was feeling more relaxed and looked forward to cycling into Inverness the following day.

Day 29, Saturday 1st July
Carrbridge to Kessock (Inverness): 35 miles.
Upon leaving the village I stopped at a traditional, old fashioned garage, where the owner kindly checked my tyres. I offered payment for his services, but he said it would be a poor day when he had to start charging people for a bit of air. He expressed concern for me, cycling on my own, and wished me well. It was a blustery day with clouds racing across a blue sky. What a difference the weather made!

I felt fit and ready for what promised to be an enjoyable and not too demanding day in the saddle. Route 7 continued on the main road, the A938. It was very quiet, because the A9 now carries most of the traffic. I didn't notice that I was gradually climbing over the Sloched Summit, a pass rising to 1,328 feet, until I was faced with a big sign advising me where I was. The sign added that I would find a hostel, a cycle shop and a ski school in the vicinity. In poor visibility it would have been another bleak place, but lady luck was smiling upon me, as was the sunshine as I bowled through the open, high roads, offering views across the northern hills. I was enjoying this!

My route took me near to the Clava Cairns, an impressive and well preserved burial site dating back four thousand years. I felt that these demanded my attention, so locking Piro, I spent an interesting half hour amongst the stones. I never had any fear that strangers would interfere with my panniers or bike, but I always took the precaution of being diligently responsible anyway.

The next important historical landmark on my route was the site of the battle of Culloden. I had visited Culloden previously, but I felt that I could not simply ignore the chance to revisit this hauntingly barren battlefield. I cycled along the meandering paths absorbing the atmosphere. This 1746 battle was the final fight between the Hanoverian government's army, led by George II's son, the Duke of Cumberland, against the troops of Bonnie Prince Charlie, who wanted to reclaim the British throne. The battle lasted but one hour. The Scottish troops suffered massive casualties, with more than 1,500 being killed or wounded compared with three hundred on the government side. Commemorative stones are to be found throughout the site of the battlefield, marking the graves of respective clans. I do not know what evidence supports the location of the sites, but clearly many visitors acknowledge their dead ancestor's burial places, as evidenced by wreaths and messages placed around the respective cairns.

Recent films and books about the battles of

Scotland's turbulent history – such as *Braveheart*, *Rob Roy* and more recently *Outlander* – have kept the public's interest in Scotland alive. Around 65,000 people pay to visit the impressive Culloden Visitors Centre, not to mention the extra 250,000 who just go to the battlefield site. You could spend a whole day there and gain enough knowledge to take a degree on the Battle of Culloden at the end of it! I didn't leave with a degree however; I left with a pair of silver earrings, crafted locally, as a souvenir.

I negotiated my way through Inverness and found my way to the Kessock Bridge, the wind whistling around me as I climbed over it. The Moray Firth was to my right, the Beauly Firth to my left, the bridge providing the link between Inverness and the Black Isle. It is renowned for being exposed to strong easterly winds and today was no exception.

The dedicated cycle path overlooking the Beauly Firth meant that I had the chance to stop and take in the views, which whetted my appetite for the final days of my trip. My two guidebooks followed roughly the same route, with one accurately describing the stage as 'brilliant'. It was an undemanding day for Piro, who still had three bars of battery when we arrived at our home for the evening.

In the dreary winter nights when I had booked my accommodation, I had paid attention to reviews good and not so good, and nearly always had an instinct about my choice. I had slipped up on this one though. Beware of plastic fruit, heavy net curtains and untidy gardens. I had to make the most of what was a very mediocre welcome. I had the impression that the couple were too old to be hosting cyclists and that they were only doing so because all payments had to be in cash. They told me that they were rushed off their feet because of the increased popularity of the '500'. This scenic route, launched in 2015, links features, towns and villages in remote areas of northern Scotland. The route has brought a gold rush to this hitherto unknown and beautiful wilderness. Accommodation is extremely scarce, providing an opportunity for people to open up bed and breakfasts to fill this gap. I couldn't help but calculate a week's takings in cash if you let out three rooms per night. It certainly beat sheep farming! I overcame my disappointment by enjoying an excellent meal at the Kessock Hotel, asking myself why I hadn't stopped there instead.

Day 30, Sunday 2nd July
Kessock to Inveran: 47miles

Following an unimpressive breakfast, I was glad to be on my way.

There was a tiny road following the Beauly Firth, which I chose instead of the proposed routes in my guidebooks. At Milton, where my road ended, I then cut up north to link in with the Cicerone E-E guide, which I would follow for the rest of the day. I was happy to be reunited with this guide, which I found indicated routes much more clearly. The red line of the route, with its blue directional arrow, stood out clearly against the buff-coloured backdrop of hills and mountains. Mileage details indicated distances from the start of each section to various towns en route; moreover, there were handy details about the route, such as advice to stock up before a long and challenging haul over a stretch of B9176 known as the Struie, which rose to 650 feet in height. My Sustrans guide followed the same route but gave no such warning, simply advising cyclists to leave route 1 and carry on over Struie on the B9176. Perhaps a small point, but for me an important one, especially thinking upon the demands on my battery.

I took the warnings seriously, stopping at Dingwall to top up both my battery and myself in one of the small family cafés which seem to be found in every Scottish town. There I met four fit young men cycling the route going south. We compared our experiences, and they gave me a huge boost by expressing what seemed to be genuine admiration for my having come so far and on my own. I said that all I had to do was to keep my battery full and to keep on pedalling! Listening to their chatter, feeling the fun and exciting vibes coming from the group, I confess to a moment of loneliness. But I soon shook off my feeling of self-pity; after all, this was something I had wanted to do my way. Perhaps it was a sign that I was tiring. I couldn't argue about my itinerary being brilliant; I had a lot to look forward to still, even this close to the finishing line.

Leaving Dingwall, I started my gradual climb over the Struie, and from my elevated position I had marvellous views over the Cromarty Firth, which was scattered with giant oil rigs. When the rigs need repairs they are towed from the North Sea to Invergordon, where the work on them is done. They made for an incongruous sight, resting on the waters amongst the otherwise rural setting.

On the other side of the road, I was aware of farmers spraying their fields, with what I knew not. It appeared to me that the potato crops were receiving a particularly heavy dose of something or other, and since that day I have been a convert to organic produce.

The climb over Struie was, as predicted, fairly challenging, but my legs easily adapted to what was asked of them. I was in heaven as I progressed through short sections of forests and wild, dramatic terrain, stopping when I felt like catching my breath or just to enjoy the space and the peace that surrounded me. Horizons stretched on and on. I had to stop to do them justice.

The wind, which was supposed to be coming

from the south, was in my face the whole day, which made the climbs lung bursting. On short, sharp climbs, how I appreciated my electric bike. I used the basic eco mode as much as I could, because in this way I would get the most out of the battery. I also had tour, sport and turbo to choose from, with gears one or two and the turbo mode being invaluable on steep hills. Without this support I could not have undertaken my adventure, but I still had to pedal!

The views from the Cadha Mor were all that had been promised, and in some way they compensated for my day in the mist over Drumochter. I tried to identify some of the Munros I could see in the distance, but I hardly had a moment to myself. I was surrounded by people the whole time! Had I had a companion, probably very few people would have ventured over to engage with me, but being a woman cyclist and on my own, I seemed to be a magnet. The viewpoint was busy with tourists and their cameras, and I was not lost for company or questions as to what I was doing. Foreign tourists were certainly swelling the coffers of both Scotland and my charity.

I swooped downhill and across the bridge into Bonar Bridge. The first thing any visitor will notice here is the impressive war memorial of a bronze, kilted soldier on a raised plinth surrounded by railings. Here were the names of the forty-six men from the area who had lost their lives in WWI and the sixteen of WWII. I passed a few moments of reflection with the fallen soldiers.

As so often happens, gazing upon the monument before me, my mind wandered to some of the other ones I had seen during my ride. There was no doubt that most villages through which I had cycled boasted a war monument. As I looked up at my kilted soldier, I wondered if he knew about his comrades who had been left in France. Of course, he couldn't have done, but I spoke to him all the same!

There are many similarly impressive commemorations to be found close to the battlefield sites in Normandy, the front line after the D Day landings, where so many soldiers lost their lives in the battle to liberate Europe. I had once thought that I knew Normandy well, but a huge slice of my education had been missing until, in 2007, I accompanied my daughter Helen and her husband Richard, his parents and granddad George, to revisit the scene of George's war. I had never before heard of Hill 112 nor of its importance in the battle for Normandy. During the last week of June 1944, a battle under the name of Epsom had raged around the villages near to the river Oden. During the fight for the bridge over the river, thousands of Welsh and Scottish soldiers gave their lives in scenes which have been described as some of the bloodiest of WWII. One section is referred to as the Scottish Corridor, where an impressive granite monument rises above tree level at Tourville-sur-Odon, topped with a lion rampart which gazes into eternity. There are similar monuments recognising the sacrifices of the Welsh regiments who also fought in the same battle. We followed the route of the battle and could hardly believe the importance of such a seemingly insignificant bridge.

Later we visited a Commonwealth War Cemetery with the Welsh dragon and Scottish saltire flags proudly flying at the entrance. We were there to honour two of George's mates, and the father of a close friend, whose Scottish father had also lost his life in the Battle of Normandy. The graves were divided into two sections. On one side a riot of daffodils seemed to dance in the wind, while on the other a blanket of heathers covered the land.

As I cast my eyes at Piro, my two flags, the dragon and the saltire, gently fluttered in the breeze, a reminder that they protected me, too, on my own very different journey – or at least, I hoped and believed so.

The sun was starting to dip and my muscles to complain as I journeyed towards Coel Mor B&B. On my way I passed the small town of Lairg. I knew about this remote market town because every August it hosts the sale of tens of thousands of sheep which come from all over the north of Scotland.

I had just one bar left on my battery as I travelled

a long, straight and level road along a glen, at the end of which, unbeknownst to me, Shangri-la awaited! My notes record that 'whereas I had paid £80 the previous evening for rubbish, this evening I paid £65 for perfection!' I was welcomed with tea and scones, which I enjoyed while taking in the views down the glen. Piro was housed in a dry barn. I later popped my ready-made meal into the host's microwave oven and enjoyed this as I read through some of the books on display for guests. I felt that I could have lingered much longer in this super establishment.

My room was beautifully decorated and warm – marvellous! And as the quality bedding welcomed me for an early night, I realised just how tired I was.

Day 31, Monday 3rd July
Inveran to Altnahara: 30 Miles

An excellent breakfast set me up for my day, which started with steady climbs through what felt like a wilderness. The cold wind continued to drive into my face, but at least it was not accompanied by rain. 'How would I have coped if I had had several days of bad weather?' I asked myself. 'With difficulty,' I answered. My bearings led me over miles of undulating, well surfaced roads, which meandered through patches of pine forests and stretches of open moorland that led my eyes to as far as I could see. I hardly saw a car and felt as though I was the only person on the planet. Sometimes I stopped and sat amongst the heather, wanting to be enveloped in the atmosphere of this rugged wilderness. There was no rush to do anything except enjoy the day.

One such rest was just before I arrived at the Crask Inn. I had just stopped on a bridge to absorb the views when I noticed some cyclists ahead of me, turning into the inn car park. One of them had noticed me on the bridge, a lone cyclist doing nothing, and cycled back to ask if everything was in order. How considerate! I assured him that all was well and finished this stage cycling with company, something which I had not done in hundreds of miles. Highland cattle wandered about the road, adding to the atmosphere.

There were several bikes parked at the inn, which has the reputation of being the remotest pub in the UK. It is a popular stage end for LEJoGers, as it offers bunk-barn accommodation and food. It also serves good coffee and light bites, and I was able to top up my battery too. There I met a couple from Wales who had a caravan not far away. They came to this remote spot every year for two months to walk, cycle and 'get away from everything'. It would have been tempting to linger, but I determined to press on towards Altnaharra, a short distance of eight miles

Both my guides mentioned the wind, and although I was cycling through undulating country with no big climbs, I was still at a high altitude. The few miles left in my day passed with a comforting glide down the only road there was, and before I knew it, I rolled into Altnaharra, population fifty. This was an early finish, as I arrived at 2.00pm, but I was tired, and glad to snuggle down out of the wind with my lunch that Sarah, my previous evening's hostess, had prepared for me.

Altnaharra had, in 1995, recorded the coldest temperature in Britain, at minus twenty-seven degrees centigrade. I had been cautioned that even in the long days of summer, temperatures could be as low as four degrees. There was a note on the door of the conservatory of my lodgings inviting guests to enter, even if it was not the official opening hours. I reasoned that in this wilderness people were prepared for all eventualities. Mandy, my hostess, soon appeared. The accommodation was as I had expected: basic, clean and welcoming, all reinforced by Mandy's warm welcome accompanied by, yet again, tea and cake. She explained that she and her husband slept in the mobile home in their garden and guests were accommodated in the house. Was it OK if I shared the night with two gentlemen who were cycling the 500? Well, err... yes, of course! My two companions duly arrived. Farmers will generally only talk about one subject, and I believe that the same can be said for cyclists. My two retired chaps were good company and totally astonished that I had come so far on my own. They offered to give Piro a clean down and check over, though I protested that I had only a couple of days left to go. We ate a substantial and very reasonably priced meal together, prepared by Mandy. There was a huge television screen in the living room so we were able to follow the highlights of the Tour de France, which was in its third day. I was supporting Geraint Thomas, the Welsh rider. My companions were far more experienced cyclists than I, and from them I learned a great deal more about the finer points of the race.

I later spoke to Hugh, who said he would soon be on his way to collect me. Besides the joy of being re-united, I was so happy that when I eventually reached John o' Groats I would not have the problem of getting home. Most cyclists have to cycle back to Thurso or Wick to get a train to Inverness, thereafter arranging onward transport. Those who can dismantle their bikes and pack them into big carrier boxes have the chance to book flights, but all of this would have to have been thought out and reserved ahead of time. Thank you, husband, for looking after me, again!

I was unable to get off to sleep as it was light until 11.30pm. I was feeling very tired, and my cold sore was still throbbing. I told myself that my tiredness was psychological because I knew the end was near and I could start to let my body relax.

Day 32, Tuesday 4th July
Altnaharra to Melvich: 38 miles
I awoke to a miracle! The sun was shining and there

was no wind. I soon donned my shorts and slathered on midge cream in preparation for what I felt would be a fabulous day in the saddle. The routes diverged at Altnaharra. The Sustrans route 1 continued straight ahead, following the A836 along Loch Loyal to Tongue and Bettyhill, whereas the E-E route turned right and followed the B871 on a quieter road with passing places. The latter was my chosen course, which would follow Loch Naver, leading to the Strath and Bettyhill. It was a memorable day, made all the more perfect by the unbelievable weather. I meandered along the shore of the loch enjoying mirrored reflections of the mountains, sky and clouds in the still waters beside me. The silence and calmness of my surroundings felt palpable. My reverie was only interrupted by the odd bleating sheep and birdsong. I wanted to capture this moment and hold it to me forever! I was truly overwhelmed.

In the hamlet of Syre I passed a small church that was constructed from corrugated iron sheets. The walls were painted white, and with the bright red roof I thought it had a Norwegian appeal to it. It is known locally as the tin church and was built in 1891 to serve the agricultural community. I was cycling through an area that had been devastated by the Highland Clearances. Between 1750 and 1860 thousands of tenant farmers and crofters were evicted from the land to allow for the introduction of sheep, which was a much more profitable crop.

The crofters' homes were destroyed so that they were unable to return to them, and the crofters forced to walk to the sea and make a living there as best they could. Consequently many people emigrated to Canada, Australia and America in search of a better life. This was the start of the destruction of the traditional clan society.

The person responsible for these notorious evictions was the Duke of Sutherland, with other Highland landowners following suit. The crofters had to wait until 1886 when, on the passing of the Crofters Holding Act, these actions became illegal and the crofters gained security and guarantees of their holdings. Upon the Duke's death, in 1833, a memorial was built on the summit of a mountain, the monument rising to 100 feet, visible for miles around. Since then there has been division in the communities, with some wanting it to be taken down, whereas others say it should be left to remind people about Sutherland's role in the Clearances.

I had wondered why a new mission church had been built to serve such a diminished agricultural community. Perhaps the passing of the 1886 Crofters Holding Act gave the community security and it was felt that better times had arrived.

How glad I was that I had been blessed with such a beautiful day. The whole world seemed to sing with me as I merrily pedalled onwards, eventually crossing the bridge where the river

Naver left the Highlands and flowed into Torrisdale Bay. It was a jaw-dropping moment, and I stopped to admire the white sandy beaches before me. Sandwiched between a backdrop of green, low cliffs and deep blue sea, it was, unquestionably, an idyllic scene. I might have expected to see people enjoying this beautiful spot, but all too soon I noticed how cold I was becoming, the north wind beginning to chill me, reminding me it was not time to linger, either to admire the view or to sit on the sand with a book.

I soon warmed up on the climb up to Bettyhill, where I stopped for coffee. I met four gentlemen, two of whom had come from New Zealand with their bikes, to meet up with their friends and to cycle from John o' Groats to Land's End. We enjoyed comparing notes, both about their trip to the UK and about the month Hugh and I had enjoyed touring New Zealand. I knew that soon opportunities for stopping in cafés and sharing chit chat would become a memory. I have never felt the need to stop for coffee when I am about my business in my local towns, and seeing cafés full of people, I sometimes wonder what the attraction is. Here in the wilderness, however, it made perfect sense.

I resisted the temptation to stop at the Strathnaver Museum, which focused on local events, especially the Clearances, because I knew that I would be there all day. However, I did make sure to have a look at the impressive Farr Stone, believed to date back to 800AD. How much of Scotland seemed to be rooted in its past, in castles, battles and history. Perhaps it was the rural, often barren surroundings I cycled through, or that its population of just over five million was mostly to be found in the Forth and Clyde central belt, but on my travels I had developed a new sense of a country that, although it has moved forward in so many ways, still holds on to its past.

I was again up against my constant enemy, as I battled into a headwind on the A836, which stretched before me, leading up and over some seriously challenging climbs. Since Bettyhill I had been reunited with Sustrans route 1, and I wondered what I had missed by having chosen the E-E route along Loch Naver. All LEJoGers were now cycling the same route along this rugged coastline, with the sea to the left and open fields stretching to far distant hills on the right. With just one battery marker remaining, I was glad to arrive at my destination, the Melvich Hotel. It was 2pm, and with more power I could have gone further. However, another seventeen miles to Thurso, the next place with accommodation, seemed a tad much, the wind having drained both me and my battery, and my body telling me to find a sheltered spot and enjoy the sun. It was too early to have access to the hotel, so I sat on the gravel path, rested against the warm wall and turned my face upwards. When had I last felt the sun truly enveloping me? As if to underline this, a lizard ran up the wall next to me, obviously enjoying the warmth as much as I.

There was nothing of interest in Melvich, but I later found my way to the tiny harbour of Portskerra, which was worth a visit, if only to think about its importance in bygone days. Here I was again in the past. On my way I had been impressed by a big memorial that commemorated men of the community who had, over the years, lost their lives at sea. On one stone, which marked a drowning in June 1890, out of eleven names listed, nine were Macdonalds. I could not imagine the impact this would have had on the community, no doubt something akin to mining disasters in the Welsh valleys.

I had been allocated a good-sized bedroom, and enjoyed what I called a 'proper pilates session'. I caught up with my paperwork and spoke to Hugh, who was well on his way to meeting me. We arranged our rendezvous for 'around 2.00pm' the following day. It was no more specific than that. I would arrive, Hugh would be there. We would return to the Melvich hotel for the evening and then motor back to Wales. The best laid plans of mice and men...

Day 33, Wednesday 5th July
Melvich to John o' Groats! 35 miles.
I was full of mixed emotions as I cycled off on my

last day. My pannier was almost empty, as I had no need for all my gear and for once was able to leave much of it in my hotel room. It was uneventful cycling, through non-descript farmland, the monotony broken only by the entrance to the Dounreay Nuclear Power Station, which is in the process of being decommissioned.

I stopped at Thurso for a break. Nobody took any interest in me; I imagine cyclists heading to or from John o' Groats are a common sight. My overriding memory of this town was of old people, pushing shopping trolleys or leaning on walking sticks, of seagulls screeching and of a bitter wind. I was glad to be on my way, and for the first time in my whole trip I could see cyclists both ahead of me and cycling towards me. We exchanged a few good-natured remarks in passing.

Five miles after leaving Thurso I arrived at Castlehill. I had seen very few trees or hedges on my way, only miles of upstanding flag stones lining the roads where hedges or fences would have been the norm. In the village I learned that, in years gone by, it had been a thriving industrial town made famous for the quarrying of flagstones that were then shipped across the world. This probably explained the use of so many of them on the wayside.

I had a final decision to make. I could follow the E-E route on the A836 and make a nine-mile detour to Dunnet Head, the true northerly point in the UK;

on the other hand I could keep on the A836 towards my goal; or I could slope off on the Sustrans route 1, which followed more rural lanes.

After some deliberation, Route 1 it was. I passed a sign for the Castle of Mey, home to the late Queen Mother. I knew that the grounds had a reputation of being worth a look and for a moment I was tempted to take an hour out for a quick visit, but I was impatient to be re-united with Hugh!

My final stop alone was to have my lunch alongside yet another impressive war memorial. Gazing up at it, I thought that during my Scottish stretch I had probably been more aware of the past than the present. In WWII it is estimated that 384,000 men of the UK lost their lives, 57,000 of whom were Scottish. I believe that this number is proportionally much greater than in the other regions of the UK. The proportion who gave their lives in WWI was greater still, with 74,000 men having died.

Impressive war memorials were in evidence in nearly every village, and in most places I passed through I had the feeling that life had not altered greatly for many years. The local shops were still doing a good trade; old fashioned local cafés could be found on every high street. I saw very few supermarkets; there were no out of town retail parks. I saw 'Yes' banners still hanging in gardens from the earlier independence vote, and as I passed I would remind myself that 'The Flower of

Scotland,' Scotland's adopted national anthem, is blasted out whenever Scotland plays in international rugby matches, paying passionate homage to Robert the Bruce, who defeated Edward II at the Battle of Bannockburn in 1314, thus re-establishing an independent Scottish monarch.

Yes, there was little doubt that, for many people, time had stood still, but for me, it was time to move on.

As I set off, I could see clifftops stretching away in the distance, so I reckoned that I still had a couple of hours to go. Had I learned nothing in a month of map reading, of paying attention to my estimated mileage, of having absorbed the instructions in my two books? What I was looking at was Duncansby Head, a few miles past John o' Groats. Either through laziness or having been overtaken by the emotion of the last few miles, I failed to register that I was upon the little port of John o' Groats until I was in the process of cycling past it. I noticed the colourful houses which line the harbour and stopped abruptly. 'I'm here!' I said. The realisation of what I had achieved cascaded over me, as a waterfall of tears poured down my face. I'd done it! My watch told me that I was probably too early for my homeward bound transport, and I thought that I might go into the official John o' Groats office to record my success. Oh, I was tempted, but more tempted to find out if Hugh had arrived, and I reasoned that he could accompany me to 'sign out' as he had when I had 'signed in' at Land's End. In a daze I freewheeled into the car park.

Similar to the car park in Cornwall, it was a big and very busy place, probably more so on such a beautiful day. I casually drifted around but could not see the car. I had been looking for the bike carrier on the back, not having realised that it could travel inside the boot. The obvious thing to do was to go to the finishing point and await collection. I removed my helmet and glasses, without which my eyesight is not brilliant, and in no time at all I was surrounded by the day trippers who, like the seagulls, seemed to be waiting for a bit of action. Money was thrust towards me and congratulations offered, with lots of questions, especially wanting to know if I really was on my own. Not for much longer, I hoped!

Suddenly I was aware of a commotion and a young lad throwing his arms around my waist, with those precious words 'Grandma!' Next Helen was beside me, giving hugs through yet more tears. But who was this lady shouting and waving a bottle over her head as she headed straight towards me? Or this bearded man wrapping me in a bear hug? No prizes for guessing who he is. I thought I had no more tears left in me!

Unbeknownst to me Helen and Thom had flown to Inverness. Thom had been granted a couple of days off school as he had been instrumental in keeping his class up to date with my ride, and it seemed only just that he should be there for the finish. Meanwhile, our friends John and Kate had been holidaying in Scotland and had altered their itinerary to include John o' Groats. It was Kate who had been waving the champagne! Last but certainly not least, Hugh had travelled up from Wales to take me home.

Helen had made a magnificent pink banner, which was to have been strung up at the finishing line, to which it was envisaged I would cycle, with friends and family awaiting my arrival. Helen said that they were all so long in the café, and in spite of her urges to get outside, it was not until Thom noticed me at the finishing point that they realised they were too late for the banner to be displayed. Nevertheless the banner was unfurled, displaying the words 'FINISH. Well done, Grandma!' plus the dates of my start and finish, mileage ridden and the Women V Cancer logo at the head.

The champagne was opened, toasts made, photos taken and yet more contributors were drawn to the racket. I was in a dream! Never, ever had I expected such a welcome! Everybody was staying at a hotel in Wick, so firstly, in the comfort of our car, I retraced the day's ride back to Melvich to retrieve my possessions. How strange it was to have all this company and chatter around me! There was a lot of news to catch up on.

During our short journey to the hotel, Hugh and

Helen remarked about how long the days were in this most northerly part of the UK and how wonderful the views that unfolded before us. I enjoyed listening to their appreciative impressions, thinking that I had been privileged to cycle through some of the very best landscapes which the UK has to offer. None of it would have meant so much if I had made the journey by car or part of an organised cycling group. Cycling LEJoG as I had done had connected me with the very soul of the towns and countryside through which I travelled. I felt that I had been at one with the people whom I had met, appreciating their regional differences, their accents and ways of life. I had embraced and enjoyed the whole experience.

I had quite a bit to report in that evening's blog. People had been following me since I had set off, and so there was a lot of attention as I neared the end. Many, many more contributions flowed in. Geoff, a member of my hill-walking club, summed it up well. 'Well done for one so young!'

This 'one so young' suddenly knew what the word 'exhaustion' meant! Yes, I felt fit and well, yes I could have turned around and cycled back home if I had really needed to, but the reality was that I had asked a lot from my body and it was telling me that it was time for a rest.

We had planned to break up our journey home with an overnight stop in Peebles, which had been booked ahead. But Hugh had asked our daughters to cancel this and to organise a hotel where I could have a bit more pampering! Consequently, at 3.00pm we drew up at a hotel/spa, its lawns and gardens seemingly invaded by women in white bath robes!

The hotel was perfect for my needs. The following day I had a massage, with most of the time being spent working on my legs, which felt as solid as tree trunks. After this, followed by a haircut and a manicure I soon felt like a new woman. As I lazed by the beautiful pool, I remember feeling so tired that I felt totally zonked. It was an effort to do anything, even to read a book. Luckily, I was told that the dress code allowed towelling robes to be worn until 5.00pm!

When we arrived home, there was an air of celebrity status around me. My charity sent me a t-shirt, recording on it my achievement, and I was pleased to have contributed over £7,000 to support their work. I was suddenly in demand as a speaker, something which I was initially hesitant about but which I came to enjoy, and at the end of most talks someone would approach me to tell me about their cycling days, or to say that I had inspired them to take on their own challenges.

I could not have achieved all that I did without the support of so many people, from the early planning stages and throughout my ride. People have lauded me with praise, but I deserve none of that. The people who deserve the praise are those fighting illnesses, of all kinds, often without complaining. All that I had to do was to keep pedalling!

I hope that you have enjoyed accompanying me on this ride. If so, you may like to follow me and Hugh as we cycle through France, Spain and Switzerland. We are both in our 70s, but we have found that age is no barrier to exploration and adventure. Hugh has taken to his electric bike in a manner which I had never thought possible. He is so much more at home tending his sheep and pushing his pen, rather than pushing pedals, and he always dreaded us having punctures. But hey, it's not a proper adventure if everything always goes according to plan!

Hugh's love, support and belief in me has, for over fifty years, remained undiminished. I carried these vibes with me as I cycled, alone, for over 1000 miles. I question whether or not I would have achieved my goal without it. Sometimes a bit of belief is all you need. After that, let your bike be your magic carpet. All that is needed is to keep the pedals turning and some good luck!

Women V Cancer is a series of cycle challenges in aid of three British charities – Breast Cancer Now, (RCN:1160558), Jo's Cervical Cancer Trust (RCN:113354/SCO41236) and Ovarian Cancer Action (RCN:1109743) – raising vital funds to fight breast, cervical and ovarian cancers. The donations you make to Women V Cancer will be distributed equally between them. The cycle challenges are organised and managed by Dream Challenges:
www.dream-challenges.com

Women V Cancer is established under GivingWorks, a charitable trust registered with the Charity Commission for England and Wales and under number 1078770.

The funds raised are restricted to use for the Women V Cancer purpose and will not be used by GivingWorks for any other purpose or as part of GivingWorks' general unrestricted funds.

If you wish to donate visit:

https://www.justgiving.com/womenvcancer